THE MAN WHO SWAM THE AMAZON

THE MAN WHO SWAM THE AMAZON

3,274 MILES
ON THE WORLD'S
DEADLIEST RIVER

BY MATTHEW MOHLKE AND MARTIN STREL

THE LYONS PRESS
Guilford, Connecticut
An imprint of The Globe Pequot Press

The Lyons Press is an imprint of The Globe Pequot Press.

10 9 8 7 6 5 4 3 2 1

Printed in the United States of America

Designed by Kirsten Livingston

ISBN 978-1-59921-358-3

Library of Congress Cataloging-in-Publication Data is available on file.

PROLOGUE

Is Martin Strel crazy? Does he have a death wish?

OK, I'll be honest. When I signed on as a kayaker to help navigate Martin Strel 3,272 miles down the Amazon River, I gave him about a 50 percent chance of survival. Myself, I gave a 90 percent chance. One thing was certain though. Martin Strel would either swim the entire Amazon River, or die trying.

The man had the whole country of Slovenia on his back, and he had too much pride to return to his homeland having failed in doing what he'd set out to do. Martin isn't the type of man who will be content riding out his waning years in some swank condo on the beach, peacefully watching the tide ebb and flow. Martin is a man of adventure. I've personally watched the man swim every mile of the Mississippi and the Paraná, and closely followed his exploits on the Danube, Yangtze, and other large rivers. But this is the Amazon. I gave him some credit for swimming those other big rivers. But still, I set the over/under at 50 percent. Is he crazy? Well, read the book and decide for yourself.

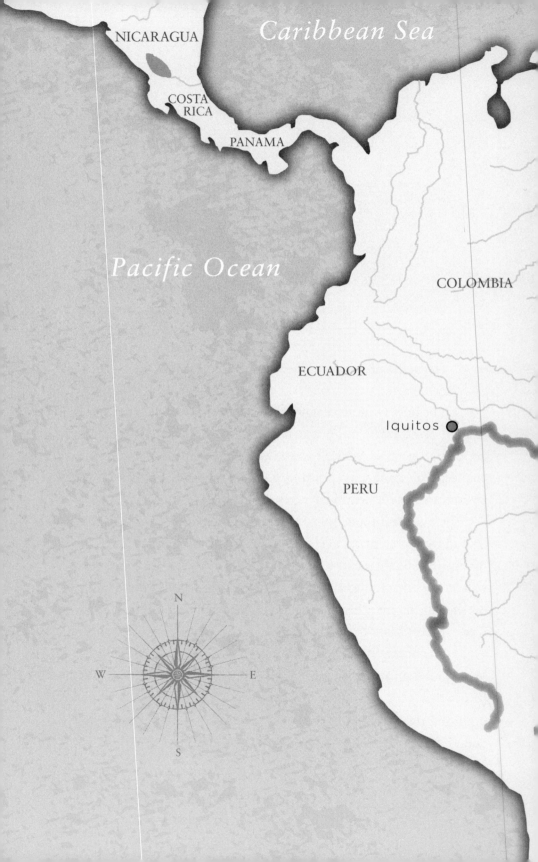

The huge, sticky, shirtless man to my immediate left is Slovenian ultramarathon swimmer Martin Strel. Beads of water drip from his forehead down his enormous frame, yet he gazes out the window, unaffected. It's already nearly a hundred degrees, but Martin doesn't allow air conditioning and won't allow us to roll down the windows. He thinks it might make him sick.

If you've ever watched Sumo wrestling, there's always that one "little guy" who charges the other fatties like a bolt of energy and ends up beating all the giants with his quickness. Well, that's the build Martin possesses, he's like the little Sumo guy. Still, as his sweaty shoulders nudge me to the edge of the bench seat and nearer to the window in the crowded van, I'm reminded he outweighs me by a hundred pounds.

I met Martin on July 1, 2002, three days before he began swimming the Mississippi River. I watched as the "world-class athlete" lazed in a lawn chair and pounded eight beers and at least six bratwurst. He was nearly fifty years old and weighed 250 pounds. His son, Borut, then a twenty-year-old pup, now expedition leader, explained to me that Martin is like a bear; he must fatten up before the swim. He'd end up shedding fifty pounds over the course of that swim.

Martin had first contacted me in 2001 because he'd read my book, *Floating Down the Country*, in which I detailed my journey down the Mississippi River on a three-dollar-per-day budget, looking for girls and a good buzz. Martin needed a few kayakers who knew the river, could give up three months of their lives, were physically capable of spending fourteen hours a day in a kayak, and would do the work for free. I guess there were only a few of us who qualified.

I wasn't informed until two weeks before we left that I'd be out of the kayak on the Amazon expedition. Instead, I'd been given the task of navigating and journal writing. Why me? For one, I'm lucky; at least Martin thinks I'm lucky. Second, and most impor-tant, I can find current. When I don't find current, Martin tears into me. It's not a pleasant experience to have Martin Strel yelling at me while boring a hole into the bridge of my nose with his eyes, so I've become pretty good at finding him current.

Lima flies by us out the window in a whir of colors and strange billboards. We'd arrived in Peru just a few hours earlier after twenty-four stressful hours of travel. Bleary-eyed and jet-lagged, we trudged forward purely on adrenaline from the lure of the Amazon. I pick up fragmented pieces of people's lives out the win-dow to my right. Girls in skintight blue skirts vigorously pump gas. Small brown men sell fresh bananas at every street corner.

Pedestrians constantly jump out in front of us, and the rule of intersections *seems* to be that whatever car is bigger and moving faster gets the right of way. In the small town in Wisconsin where

I live, everyone stops at an intersection and is afraid to be the first to go. Here, they all go at once, then honk. A frantically crying woman with wildly frizzled hair and demon eyes waves her hands at each car as she walks in the lane against incoming traffic. I have a strong premonition she won't survive the day.

"Smell today," Martin tells us as we reenter the Lima airport. "Tomorrow will be different smell. Tomorrow will be jungle." We'd landed at this same airport just four hours ago and transferred thousands of pounds of equipment across town to a hotel, only to bring it all back again to catch another flight to Pucallpa.

Martin is beaming. He enjoys strutting around with his entourage, all of us in matching team uniforms loaded with European team sponsors. We're a pretty fierce bunch, ready to take on the jungle. At the airport, Martin has two goals: beer and food.

Martin's a fun guy when he's not swimming a river. He likes music, he enjoys the sight of a pretty woman, he likes to laugh, and he loves to have a beer or glass of wine with his friends. On the other hand, when he's in the midst of a swimming expedition, Martin is, for the most part, unapproachable. His mind goes somewhere else, and he turns into a machine that just eats, sleeps, and swims.

Personally, I enjoy those rare moments before and after a swim when I can spend time with the real Martin Strel, before he puts his mind away into some far-off compartment, locks the door, and becomes Martin Strel the swimming robot.

January 26—Pucallpa, Peru

At the landing strip in Pucallpa, we're surrounded by aggressive looking men on motorbike taxis who all direct us to get in. "There are dangerous people here," Martin warns us. "Stay near." The men prove to be friendly—just excited to see gringos.

"I like to drink. I like to dance. I like to make the fookie-fookie," our wild-eyed driver tells us in broken English as he makes a sexual hand gesture. Pucallpa is a party town with a care-free attitude. One man lies naked on the dirt by the side of the road, fully exposed to the world. Another man buys ice cream dressed with only a thin blanket slung over his shoulder.

During lunch at a damp, riverside bodega, we have a hard time understanding the owner over the loud disco music pumping out of a small boom box on a nearby rickety table. She retrieves her young son who gives us two choices, "dog or pig." We all choose pig. In the afternoon, I'm unsuccessful in my wild goose chase to acquire a fishing pole. There is no such thing as a fishing pole on the upper Amazon. They use their hands to throw a line.

The team is taking malaria pills, but nothing is 100 percent effective. Natives tell us that some of us may go home with "just a little malaria." Martin is very concerned about the malaria medications we're all taking. He reprimands American river guide Jamie Zelazny for taking the medication his doctor had recommended.

"This isn't North America, this is South America. It is very different. Don't listen to doctor. I am your doctor." From handling the baggage to choosing the seats on the plane, Martin takes control of every situation he finds himself in.

The mayor and other city officials take us out for a fabulous dinner of carne asada, pork, and fried bananas. With concerned faces, they warn Martin about many of the dangerous animals that he will encounter on the river, such as crocodiles, anacondas, piranha, and candirú. Martin just smiles and nods his head with a look to mean something like, "I know something you don't know."

January 27—Atalaya, Peru

The barrel-chested Martin Strel steps off our twelve-passenger jungle plane amidst a throng of puzzled Peruvian faces. They'd seated us according to weight on the tiny plane from Pucallpa, big guys in front, small guys in the back. The two-hour flight has no schedule; the plane takes off whenever they find enough people to fill it.

Atalaya is a jungle town. The only way to reach it is by boat or plane. Everything is alive with green as the jungle tries to retake the city. "I love the smell of the jungle," a sweat-drenched Martin declares as he exits the plane with his new Peruvian guitar in his hand.

The founder of Atalaya was Juan Santos Atahualpa. He was an Apu Inca who led 50,000 Ashaninkan Indians against the Spaniards in 1742. "There will be no slavery," he declared, and they gave up their lives to ensure the future freedom of these same Incan descendants who gaze on Martin today. He's the first white man some of these warm people have ever seen and is twice as big as most of them.

We have dinner in a shaded hut on top of the largest hill in town. After a few beers Martin lies in a hammock and listens to some peaceful Peruvian music while three chickens roost around him. "I love the jungle," he tells us with a smile. He had visited Atalaya a few years earlier to exchange gifts with some tribal chiefs and shamans in order to be granted permission to pass through certain remote areas of the river. In doing so, he had fallen a little in love with the city.

Martin has developed a thing for the new machete he purchased from a native last evening and has been gleefully carrying it around the village with him all day. His behavior somehow childlike, innocent. I've been relishing these last few days of enjoying South America with Martin, because I know that the moment he dips a toe into that Amazon River, he will transform into an entirely different man. Martin the man is my friend. Martin the swimmer is just a guy I work for, and I know that the moment he flips the switch, he'll be a tough man to deal with for the next seventy days.

Martin is given the honor of raising the flag of the city for its annual holiday. Children are permitted to throw water balloons all day to commemorate the Incan battle that took place in 1742. After the ceremony, the mayor takes us on a jungle tour in his jeep. Curious Peruvian faces peek out of every hut along the terribly-rutted dirt road.

After driving deeper and deeper into the jungle for two hours the road becomes too rough to continue. The mayor leads us on a short hike down a steep hill that opens to a crystal-clear stream full of tiny, colorful fish. The day is unbearably hot, and although hesitant at first, we all strip down into our underwear and jump into a large pool in the brook. After leaping off a few small cliffs near a waterfall, Martin pauses for a quick can of tuna in his tighty-whiteys. He's just like a kid, laughing, swimming, joking, and playing. The mayor shows us some edible plants, and we lounge around our little secret paradise all afternoon, having a blast, but getting burned to a crisp.

Later in the day, Martin does some training in the Amazon. Despite numerous warnings, he decides it's too hot for his wetsuit. We follow in a peké peké (pronounced *peck E peck E*), a motorized dugout canoe that is three feet wide and thirty feet long. Martin swims like a champion, impressing the media representatives among the nine onboard the peké peké who'd never seen him swim, but the boat ride is a nightmare. Floating chunks of debris are everywhere, the currents are unpredictable, and we have way too many people in the canoe, many of whom have no idea how to counterbalance such a tippy craft. With two people in a canoe, the guy in the back can lean a little to his right when he sees the guy in the front lean a little to the left. We have nine people packed into a canoe, half of whom are greenhorns who don't realize that every time they lean over to snap a photo or comment on how beautiful the Amazon is, the entire boat shifts and the brown water rises to within a half inch of the gunwale of the boat. Looking to the shoreline, I unlace my shoes and put a hand on either side of the canoe, trying to anticipate the movements of those in front of me so I can counterbalance the boat. At first many of the occupants laugh at me, but after water splashes in from the right side causing everyone to gasp and quickly lean left, the entire boat had assumed a similar position.

For the last year I've been that cocky bartender who's "going down the Amazon." Every guy in the bar had a million questions and I was always happy to oblige. I loved to see their faces light up in disbelief as they imagined traveling through the most dangerous jungle in the world. My chest puffed out proudly as they shook their heads and returned to their beer mugs as I went to serve the next customer.

I had been on the Amazon River for exactly ten minutes and was scared out of my wits. The expedition hasn't even started yet, and part of me already wishes I was safe back behind the bar again. I'd expected the headwaters of the Amazon to be fairly gentle, but it's already bigger and wilder than the Mississippi at her worst. Again I scan the shoreline, remembering not to fight the current but to let it take me. I expect to drift at least two miles in order to make the half-mile swim back to shore.

I'm fairly sure I can make it, but not so sure of the others. They seem to be more concerned about their cameras getting wet than their bodies. With all nine of us motivated by fear and working together now, we manage to keep the thing afloat, but I vow never to enter another peké peké.

The solar rays here are more extreme than most of us have ever experienced. After a full day in the direct sun, some of us on the team have a rough evening as we deal with sunburn and a little heat exhaustion.

We see our first Amazon woman in Atalaya. She's barefoot, exhausted, incredibly ugly, and has thunderous thighs and calves. She walks with a machete in one hand and a long stick in the other. I guess from her appearance that she may have walked as many as ten miles to come into the village to buy supplies.

The mayor and other local government officials warn Martin of a potential problem. Strong whirlpools have overturned many large boats at the confluence of the Ucayali and Pachitea Rivers. Villagers are still abuzz about one boat that capsized, resulting in the loss of 170 lives. Many of these people lived in Atalaya. The team makes plans to send a boat ahead to scout the area to provide Martin with the least dangerous route.

January 29—Atalaya, Peru

The people of Atalaya are curious, but mind their own business. They never take more than one quick peek at us. They're poor, but will give away anything they possess as a symbol of friendship. This is expected to be reciprocated, however, and anything a new friend sees on you can be considered fair game.

We haven't seen any people over the age of fifty. It's possible they die off from lack of proper medicine or because of the harsh climate. Little dogs run free all over town. They're timid, sickly, and gangly looking, but seem to have a sense of purpose when they do get off their butts to go walking around. Usually, they just lie around, each occupying its own street corner, looking for scraps of food. They crap right in the middle of the street, and most have constant diarrhea, some have sore, infected looking asses, and crapping looks painful.

In the evening, Martin is invited to attend a special ceremony among Ashaninkan chieftains. They have agreed to give him their blessing to swim through the Provincia of Ucayali. The climax of the meeting occurs when an indigenous woman with a painted face offers a spirited song to pray to her gods to offer Martin protection. At the end of the song she surprises all in attendance by taking Martin's hand and having him join her in a ritual dance. Martin seems a little shy and awkward, but he does his best to keep up a good smile and follow the native woman's lead to perform the ceremonial dance.

Some of the natives express great concern over the dangers in this part of the river. The candirú is a small fish that is attracted to the smell of urine and blood. It darts into a human orifice such as an anus, vagina, or even penis, erects a razor-sharp spike to hold it in place, then latches onto an artery and feeds off blood. Once it has lodged into this cozy position, it's nearly impossible to remove except by surgery. It's by far the creature most feared by Amazon locals, much more than the piranha. We've brought some condoms along to use as a precautionary device, and an experienced river man has also suggested to Martin that he supplement these with lemon juice as a natural repellent. Crocodiles are also very common here and Martin will be in great jeopardy each time he swims in dark, still waters away from the fast current. This will make getting into and out of the river extremely dangerous. Anacondas and piranhas are also attracted to the slower moving water.

We've heard a few reports of banditos who do some smuggling downstream from here, and as a result, Martin is looking to acquire some guns. Martin listens to all of these warnings soberly, nods his head a few times, and asks a few questions, but not once does he give the appearance of being the least bit concerned.

I ask Borut about this later and he tells me that Martin will make friends with the animals of the river over the course of the seventy-day swim. By the end of the trip, they will accept him completely as just another big fish. Martin believes he's invincible to the predators of the Amazon.

January 30—Atalaya, Peru

Training in the Amazon has given Martin a painful sunburn as he acclimates to the climate. Our support boat carrying supplies from Pucallpa has still not arrived, and we're unable to make radio contact. Our last report indicated they were approximately sixty-two miles downstream and struggling with some unpredictable river conditions. We make plans to send another boat to meet them on the following day as we have some essential supplies on board.

The local people have an interesting way of sharing drinks here. One large bottle of beer is shared by up to eight people using only one glass. The first person in line pours as much as they want, passes the bottle, drinks the beer and passes the glass. The bottle rarely makes it around the group more than one time. It gives me a whole new mental image of the song "99 Bottles of Beer on the Wall." The locals always buy the first beer, or so I thought, then the beers keep coming and coming and of course we always get stuck with the bill.

January 31—Atalaya, Peru

A tense mood hangs over the team today. This is always the case in the waning hours before starting an expedition. Many small details need to be resolved and new problems are always coming up at the last minute. Martin, Borut, and Jamie go on a scouting mission to find our support boat. After weaving through a maze of islands and floating debris in a speedboat, they locate it sixty-miles downstream. They transfer some essential supplies and delegate Jamie to stay with the support boat and help navigate an all-night trip upstream that is projected to reach Atalaya at 5:00 AM. Martin will begin swimming at 8:00 AM.

Borut, the expedition leader, is taking all of the logistical burdens of the trip on his own shoulders. He prefers to handle the minutest of details himself, rather than delegate, and has been working on the computer all night for the last three nights. The arrival of director John Maringouin and his lead cinematographer Paul Marchand from the *Big River Man* documentary crew has also changed the mood of the team. It can be hard to get one's work done when blinded by a bright light and scrutinized by the camera lens.

One of the hardest parts of these expeditions is knowing you'll have to live on a boat in close quarters with strangers for the next seventy days. The first meeting with each new roommate is a feeling out process to see how we might get along.

I'm a little tentative around the film crew at first, especially John. Maybe it's my bias against the whole Hollywood scene, but he seems a little too slick for me, walking around in his plaid shirt, oversized sunglasses, whistling tunes from the seventies, and talking about people's vibes while seeming to be completely in control of the situation at all times. Many of the scenarios from the *Jackass* movies were his brainchild, a fact that has me on my toes as well. By the hottest part of the day, he removes his plaid shirt revealing a white wife-beater tank top, and I can faintly detect a hick Louisianan accent as he inquires about my chewing tobacco. Ok, so maybe we aren't that different. I might actually be able to be friends with this guy.

Having doctors on the boat would seem to be a comfort, but I've been scared to go to the doctor's office since I was a kid. My last visit was in 1989. The doctors from the telemedicine team also come equipped with their own set of ulterior motives. Dr. Mateja de Leonni Stanonik and Dr. Rifat Latifi are using Martin's swim down the Amazon as a forum to tell the world about telemedicine, a way for doctors around the world to have live conferences to treat patients in the most remote of jungle locations. They're carrying hundreds of thousands dollars of state-of-the-art equipment, and already had one bag stolen from the airport that was valued at about $50,000. Today they requested we all undress so they might get before and after pictures of us in case one of us might acquire some sort of bite or other skin infection. The whole idea of having before and after pictures taken of me makes me feel like some sort of guinea pig.

As I sit in the sweaty computer lab at the hostel, tiny green lizards run up and down the walls around me. Team members are frantically approaching me every few minutes, "Where is Martin? Where is Borut? Where is the boat?" The bathroom seems to always be occupied, as several members of the team, me included, are already having stomach problems before the trip has even begun.

One major cause of contention among the team is the acquisition of buckets of blood to use as a deterrent against predators. Personally, I'm not sold on the idea that throwing entrails over the other side of the boat if Martin is attacked by piranhas or other predators will be enough to divert the attack, but both Borut and Martin insist the plan is solid. The contentions arise over the logistics of the blood buckets. Where do we store them?

At evening time, Borut and I acquire about two gallons of blood from the local pig killer, but then find ourselves standing around outside our Atalayan hostel, arguing about whose room we'll keep the blood in. We finally pay a man the equivalent of one dollar to keep the slimy bucket in a storage shed across the street.

Martin will begin swimming at 8:00 tomorrow morning. Tonight he will attempt to sleep three or four hours as he mentally prepares himself for the longest and most dangerous swim in the planet's history.

February 1—Amazon jungle near Taurapa, Peru

A tone of chaos dominates the morning of the expedition's start. The 8:00 AM start is fast approaching, and Jamie has still not shown up with the support boat. We hire another boat to take the team and equipment downstream to meet it, but an argument arises between Martin and the owner of the boat. The man wants 200 sol, the Peruvian currency, and Borut is only willing to give him 100. A multimillion-dollar expedition is being held up over the equivalent of thirty dollars.

After Borut finally convinces the man of a compromise, a tremendous downpour begins. The team is forced to store hundreds of thousands of dollars in satellite equipment in a stinky bathroom by the riverfront. Hundreds of soaking-wet Atalayans brave the weather and slight delay to cheer Martin on from the waterfront. "The jungle is crying because you are leaving." The words of one local sum up the mood in Atalaya as Martin prepares to begin his seventy-day swim in a heavy downpour.

Martin enters the river about an hour and a half after his scheduled starting time. He shoots away from shore so fast that the small escort boat struggles to keep up with him in the heavy current. He swims the first three hours in total silence, stopping once to utter a single word, "Drink." The six people in the escort boat stare in disbelief as he quickly guzzles a pint of energy drink, then goes back to his powerful freestyle stroking. They're all a little disappointed, having waited for hours for him to pop his head up and talk to them, proving that he's human. They'd only been gifted one word. An hour later, they're treated again. "How many kilometers?" followed by a grunt, then more swimming.

Martin becomes a little more vocal in the late morning, stopping twice to give Jamie an earful. Jamie had taken his eyes off the river for a few seconds to take a few pictures of the beautiful scenery. "Jamie, this is not holiday. This is not tourist boat. One mistake, we all go home." Grimacing, he says these last words with a throat-slashing gesture.

Jamie had volunteered to take over my morning shift after an all-night boat trip because I was struggling with a severe bout of diarrhea. He does an excellent job directing Martin into the fastest possible current while under considerable pressure to navigate during the all-important first half day of the expedition. After draining my whole box of Imodium, I start a five-day regimen of prescription drugs, grab a bucket and some toilet paper, and hop in the escort boat to start my first Amazon shift with Martin.

It's impossible for Martin to swim and think about swimming at the same time. The best analogy I can offer is that while swimming, Martin is outside of his body. It's the only way he can withstand the pain and last every day through the long hours. I watch him swim, I see his body moving, but his glazed, unfocused eyes show that he's really not there.

As navigators, our jobs are simple. Look for the fastest current, avoid whirlpools, and blow a whistle every time danger comes. But, at the same time, I must use discretion. To blow my whistle and bring Martin back to the pains of the present moment pisses him off, so I do that as little as possible.

We use GPS and detailed topo maps to track our progress and make decisions about where to stop and what side of islands to travel on. We also prepare drinks and carry bananas for Martin and provide an outlet for him as scapegoats for when he needs to blow off steam.

A moist morning surrenders to a tranquil afternoon of light breezes and mysterious animal noises. The rain is gone, the sun is covered in clouds, and a tone of adventure captivates the team. The foothills of the Andes are shrouded in cotton balls as Borut and I take turns paddling a small support boat with local guides Geraldo, Arturo, and Jarvez.

While swimming near a sloppy bank shaded by huge Lupuna trees, Martin disturbs a six-foot long alligator that quickly breaks its slumber and disappears below the dark waters. A freshwater dolphin magically appears. The first time it porpoises we're afraid of what strange creature lurks below the dark waters. When we realize it's a dolphin, a wave of joy sweeps over the whole team. The dolphin leads the swimmer downstream. We also see our first naked natives, albeit at a great distance.

In the late afternoon, we finally encounter the *Cielito Lindo*. The thing is chugging along at approximately two miles per hour against the fast current. At ninety-two feet long and three stories high, the awkward boat looks like a big white rectangle with a giant rainbow painted on the side. We transfer our essentials and climb aboard our new home.

Despite many whirlpools and floating debris, Martin muscles his way through sixty-three difficult miles today. He quits his poker face to express some rare happiness at the team dinner. After a successful first day on the river, he's smiling and joking with us, constantly filling our glasses with more San Juan cerveza. I'm bummed out because my antibiotics do not permit me to partake. Mostly though, I'm stunned. In three expeditions, I've never seen Martin so relaxed after a day of swimming. Maybe he's getting softer in his old age, or maybe the presence of the film crew is making him more personable. I'm not sure, but I like it anyway, and hope it will continue throughout the expedition.

After dinner, the little party ends and the team sets up a

makeshift office in the mess hall of the boat. We all grab a different corner of the room and quietly go to work commemorating the day with pictures and stories. Even the usually boisterous, often slightly buzzed Bojan Premelc (aka Pibi) is silently concentrating, selecting a small portfolio of pictures from the hundreds he'd taken to represent the historical day. A large, wild-looking man who looks more and more like a grey-bearded castaway as expeditions progress, Pibi has the perfect psychological makeup to complete such an endeavor. He's usually found with a camera around his neck, a beer in one hand, and a cigarette with an inch of ash in the other. We were part of the Paraná River expedition together, and other than Borut and Martin, he's the only one I'm completely sure of on this one.

February 2—Amazon Jungle near Bolognesi, Peru

Although they acknowledged its beauty, most conquistadors looking for El Dorado hated the Amazon. Some called it, "Green
Death," and considered it a place that one entered, but rarely left.
So far the team has appreciated the beauty of the Amazon, but
we've yet to see her dark side.

A morning cloudburst is replaced by another day of favorable
conditions as Martin begins his second day of swimming. Temper-
atures remain in the eighties and the sun is covered for 95 percent of
the day. Martin capitalizes on today's good weather by swimming an
astounding seventy-five miles. He starts the day in a business-like
fashion and keeps up his quiet demeanor for the entire twelve hours
of swimming. With Martin, an uneventful day is a rarity, but it's a
good thing. Usually there is some unforeseen disaster that holds the
team back and causes Martin to lose precious miles.

We alarm Martin of several dangerous whirlpools and a never-
ending array of half-submerged trees with sharp blows from our
safety whistles, but none of these obstacles impede his progress.
The support boat is greeted by curious villagers at the small
settlement of Bolognesi, the only location to acquire gasoline for
335 miles between Atalaya and Pucallpa. We're surprised to discover it's common for the natives to throw their garbage in the
river. Every settlement is followed by scattered plastic wrappings
for the next mile or so downstream.

The first few days of most expeditions are usually dominated
by nightmarish bouts of confusion in which time is lost that will
put the team behind the eight ball from the start. It usually takes
a week or so to get into a routine on a long distance excursion. So
far, every break has gone in Martin's favor. The weather has been
cooperative, the team is solid and in fair health, and logistical

problems have been solved quickly. I can't see Martin keeping up this pace for seventy days, and I have a feeling that our fortunate day today will be a high water mark that we may never reach again. A guy can't swim seventy-five miles through the jungle in a day that easy, can he?

We see two more small dolphins and a tiny alligator today. Anchoring for the night in front of a small village, we are instantly surrounded by small children. The high water has caused massive erosion in the area, and four families from the village have recently lost their huts as the Amazon widens her banks.

Drs. Rifat Latifi, and Mateja de Leonni Stanonik, directors of the Amazon Virtual Medical Team announce today that Martin is doing great physiologically and is in good spirits after administering his twice-daily physical examinations. A few of us are suffering from some stomach ailments. I'm on antibiotics, and unfortunately won't be able to have a beer for eight days. Dr. Latifi told me that 100 percent of the people from Atalaya have parasites. The memory of the dogs with diarrhea stays with me.

Martin has gone to bed early to prepare for his 5:00 AM alarm. Borut is outside dancing and swatting at mosquitoes as he sets up a bug net in his attempt to defy Mother Nature and upload the website. The ability to transmit news stories from our jungle location, hundreds of miles from the nearest civilization is crucial. It's frustrating for all of us on the support team to be cut off from our family and friends, and Borut's nightly transmission is our only link to planet earth. We're so far away from everything out here, it's as if the earth has swallowed us up, and every day we travel deeper and deeper into her belly. As he transmits, Pibi and I stand off to the side, anxiously hoping our messages made it through this time, feeling like David Bowie's Major Tom trying to contact ground control.

February 3—Near Iparia, Peru

A blanket of early morning fog makes for navigational hell this morning. We can only see a few meters out in front of Martin and sometimes by the time we notice some hazardous debris it's nearly too late. Martin is angry at me for forgetting the machete. We've heard of a few boats being pirated in this area, and although a blade won't do much against a gun, we hope it might act as a deterrent of some kind, or at least give us a little more peace of mind.

The scariest part about the morning isn't just the absence of visibility, it's all the strange jungle noises we can hear but can't identify. Sometimes the shoreline appears in a gap in the fog, and then it's gone again. I suddenly realize, *hey, this is the jungle. There are things out here that could kill me in about ten seconds.* A quick wave of fear passes through me, then it's gone just as quickly as it comes, but I hear another strange sound in the fog, feel the eyes upon me that may or may not be there, and the fear returns. When the fear comes like this, I just have to wait for it to pass. I know the others on the boat feel it too, but I can't talk to them about it. It wouldn't be right.

At 8:00 the fog lifts, but a new problem arises. Erosion from the high water is cutting huge chunks of land away from the bank. Monstrous Lupuna trees are being timbered into the water. We pass another village that has lost several homes to the Amazon in the previous days. One tree falls about fifteen meters from Martin, and we make a navigational decision to stay away from cut banks for the duration of the trip, even though they usually possess the best current.

Sometimes we have a hard time deciphering our exact location on the maps. A village is either entirely gone, or maybe three miles downstream, on the other bank from where it is on the map. Apparently, when a town finally crumbles into the river, the people just pick up what they have left and find another suitable location for the settlement. The Amazon changes so much that our six-year-old charts are already severely outdated.

This morning Martin is sucked away from the main channel and into a chute between two islands. Several huge trees are hung up in the mud. Sometimes we see only a few branches sticking up, but beneath the water is the entire thing, complete with partially torn-off limbs waiting to impale the swimmer or entangle him to a point where he would be glued to the submerged base.

In the afternoon, we hear a giant sucking noise as Martin passes a jagged point of land. A huge whirlpool appears out of nowhere, threatening to swallow the swimmer, but he manages to power his way through. We carry rescue equipment and try to keep the boat close to him, but the motor has been having trouble today and sometimes it stalls on us for minutes at a time, leaving the swimmer as many as fifty yards out ahead of us. This is a tremendously scary situation as we have no way of communicating dangerous water to him or intervening should an emergency occur.

Strong currents aid Martin again today to the tune of seventy-one miles. I'm impressed with the mileage Martin is covering on this trip, but still am pessimistic about the future. He's getting all the lucky breaks and hasn't had any major setbacks.

While swimming, Martin has been all business over the first three days. He swims and occasionally grunts, but rarely talks. Sometimes I see his lips moving like he's talking to himself, but he doesn't talk to us much, and when he does it's always just a request for time, drink, or a mileage total. Watching him swim, I can't help but imagine that somehow in his mind it's not so much that he's swimming toward the ocean, but more like he's swimming away from something else. Borut tells me that Martin's father was especially hard on him, beating him severely on a few occasions. Martin could be swimming to impress his father, or swimming to get away from his father, I'm not sure.

Near dusk, we find a nice place near a small clearing in the jungle to dock the main boat for the evening. The doctors and Hollywood guys go on shore to explore. They quickly reappear, running back to the boat as we see a man with a rifle emerge from the thick green vegetation behind them, yelling something indecipherable, followed by three ladies with machetes. When they see the boat, they all reverse back into the jungle as fast as they appeared, we presume to get reinforcements. We quickly untie the boat and head downstream. As we motor away, we see the man returning to shore with his machete toting entourage. They wave us away in a frantic two-armed gesture, to be understood as, "go away and never come back."

We find another suitable sleeping spot on the other bank, and are greeted by a family of five, packed in a large dugout canoe. The three shy children wear second hand shirts with American slogans. One little girl sports a pink shirt that reads, "Dressed to Kill." The man invites us to his hut, and a few of us go ashore to check it out. The bamboo-thatched house on a small clearing of pounded down dirt has many small chickens, a three-legged dog, and bananas frying for dinner over an open fire. The doctors come ashore to look at one of the children while the rest of us do our best to communicate in our broken Spanish to the man and his wife.

The team is nervous about reaching the confluence of the Pachitea and Ucayali Rivers. Not only is it home to some deadly whirlpools at the confluence, it's also known as one of the most pirated areas on the Amazon. We'd like to send a scouting crew ahead to check for the safest route, but are afraid to send them too far away from the safety of the larger boat. After a lengthy discussion, we decide to ready a small boat to scout the area slightly ahead of the main boat and try to time the crossing for the early morning hours.

February 4—Pachitea Confluence, Peru

Alfredo Chavez, the lead Peruvian guide and interpreter wakes Martin up with loud knocking at 3:30 AM. "Marteen, Marteen." He sounds a little drunk.

Jamie and I are in the next room over, and the commotion wakes us up as well. Wondering how anyone could possibly be crazy enough to knock on Martin's door at this hour, we attempt to listen to the muffled conversation through the thin wall. We can only acquire bits and pieces, but apparently the steering column in the boat is damaged, and the secondary motor is almost caput.

"What time is it?" responds a weary swimmer. He was planning on starting a little early today, but not this early. He seems to not fully understand what Alfredo is telling him.

The conversation ends and we all go back to sleep, but an hour later the alarm is ringing.

Martin starts swimming just before sunrise to get through the disreputable confluence area as early as possible. Borut goes ahead a mile or so with a Peruvian guide, picks out a safe route, and radios back to us with his directions. The current is swift and there are a few whirlpools, but we make it through without incident, in fact, we don't even see another boat. By late morning we're several miles past the confluence when the wind picks up and the big boat begins to have some major steering problems.

As I start my afternoon shift in the boat escorting Martin, the *Cielito Lindo* is depending on the current to float her into Pucallpa. Before long, the steering is completely gone. Martin is swimming much faster than the wind-impeded ship, and we watch her slowly disappear as we round a lazy bend in the river. It bounced from bank to bank, out of control, with glass breaking and the crew being heaved from side to side. Eventually, it found a shallow spot and was stuck in the mud for almost twenty-four hours. While the big boat sends out an SOS, Martin swims out of radio contact with the smaller escort boat.

Borut makes a decision for Martin to continue swimming with the escort boat and for me not to inform him of the trouble, at least not right away. He has enough to worry about already, and the main goal of the expedition is for Martin to cover as many miles as possible each day. We'd figured they'd be free in an hour or so and able to catch up, but now we're all alone.

With no support boat, our only option is to try to make it to Pucallpa. As darkness sets in after a long day of swimming, the lights of Pucallpa finally begin to twinkle in the distance, giving us all a sense of safety. Although they look near, my GPS tells me they're still six miles away.

Our false sense of security quickly vanishes when the whining hum of a boat motor announces we have company on the river. Suddenly a light from a speedboat appears upstream and another downstream. These boats are fast, and unlike anything we've seen on the Amazon thus far. Our Peruvian guides warn us to kill all the lights and be very quiet. "Shush, narco, assaulto," Jarvez hisses at us, saying the first two words with an outstretched pointer finger to his lips and extending his finger out toward us into the shape of a gun for the last word. These Peruvian guides are tough as nails and say very little over the course of the day. If they're scared, I'm scared.

We do as we were told and sit bobbing in the darkness, unsure of what to do next. We've heard of the narcos, drug traffickers who work this stretch of the river, serving as middlemen between the jungles of Peru and the cartels of Colombia, and they don't like anybody to get in their way. The two speedboats come together, stop, and turn off their motors.

We hear men conversing quietly in Spanish from the other side of the river but can't make out what they're saying. They'd killed their lights now and the silhouettes of their boats are just barely visible against the thick jungle backdrop as they slowly drift downstream at about the same rate as us. I figure that if we can barely see them, they will almost surely not be able to see us if we're quiet enough.

Jarvez, Gerardo, and I lift and pull our paddles in silence to try to move closer to the shoreline and distance ourselves from the narcos as Martin swims silently on the other side of the boat. He looks a little scared too.

The final six miles are done without illumination as we paddle blind and listen for rough water ahead while Martin swims cautiously nearby. The meeting of the speedboats is brief and we hold our breath as both boats fire up their motors and turn the lights back on. I worry that one might randomly drive directly past us and light us up with their beams, but they both speed off the same way they'd come. I watch as the lights get dimmer and dimmer and the motor hum lower and lower until the river is again ours alone.

Martin reaches solid ground in a seedy part of town with nothing except his wetsuit. The four of us do not have any money, and I'm dreading the idea of squeezing together in a fourteen-foot flat-bottom boat to sleep in a questionable area. There are some strange looking characters beginning to take notice of us on the waterfront and Jarvez strikes up a conversation with them in order to pacify them. He says something in Spanish, gestures at Martin, and they all laugh a little and seem a little friendlier. I can still see that Jarvez is apprehensive, and I'm a little scared too. There's no way I'm sleeping in this little boat with four men. Martin has already fallen asleep.

Choosing the tougher looking of the two Peruvians, I ask Gerardo, a thin, older gentleman, to stay with Martin while the burly young Jarvez and I fearfully walk to town to look for some friendly faces. "Is it dangerous here?" I ask in Spanish.

"Sí, muy peligroso aquí," he affirms. I cover my gringo hair with a sombrero, and walk away from the waterfront with a purposeful stride. We get to a main street and see a taxi but have no money, so Jarvez exchanges his sombrero for a motorcycle taxi ride to the hotel we stayed at last week. I know that sombrero meant a lot to him, he never took it off.

Our aim is to look for Lady Henderson and her father Carlos, who've helped us much throughout the trip. Lady has acted as our interpreter for much of the expedition. She's also a very beautiful, intelligent, and thoughtful young woman of twenty-four, and has gained the respect of the team with her competence at finding us solutions for scores of little problems that have arisen throughout the expedition. Lady and Carlos have taken on the responsibility of presenting us in both Pucallpa and Atalaya and helping Martin to build rapport with other leaders of the area.

We find the hotel, a five star place, and of all the weird luck in the world, the darn Super Bowl is on the TV in the lobby. It's late in the fourth quarter and the Colts are ahead of the Bears. Wow, I've never missed a Super Bowl in my life and here it's the fourth quarter of a great game, and I don't even care. I can't even care. I suddenly realize just how far away from America I am.

We locate the Hendersons with help from the front desk, they show up in ten minutes to pick us up, and we race back to the waterfront to wake up Martin. Carlos puts the escort boat in a safe place for the night and we're back in the finest hotel in the entire jungle. In the last two hours we've gone from penniless vagabonds sleeping in a small boat to lounging in the lap of luxury. Gerardo and Jarvez insist on staying with the boat, but we drag them off to the hotel where we all enjoy a moonlit swim in the pool and some cable television. Martin takes a room for himself and I squeeze into another with the two Peruvians. I've learned a lesson in humility from these guys. They work all day, seven days a week for the equivalent of fifty dollars, refuse water and food when offered, never complain, and are always smiling.

February 5—Pucallpa, Peru

A frustrated Martin Strel awakes early to look for news about the support boat. It's too dangerous to continue without a support boat, and we have serious communication barriers. The day is essentially lost as Martin comes to the realization he has no option other than to patiently wait for the team to be rescued and the boat repaired.

Martin loosens up a little at lunch. He has a few beers and tells us all a story of when he was seven years old and dammed a little creek by his home in order to create a small swimming pool. Young Martin would often come home a crispy red from hours in the sun, and be soundly whipped by his father.

We're treated to dinner by the Presidente of the Regional De Ucayali, Dr. Jorge Velasquez Portocarrero. Since Martin has no clothing, he dines in the fancy restaurant barefoot, with a borrowed San Juan Cerveza T-shirt and a pair of Bermuda shorts. Dr. Portocarrero is leading a new political movement known as the "Parrot Party." One of their goals is to revitalize the waterfront at Pucallpa and build a beautiful boulevard.

When the curious Presidente politely asks Martin his age, he responds, "I'm more than thirty-five. I'm not old but I have been a long time in this world."

As we wait on the waterfront for news from the boat, Martin even starts joking with me, hiding with another radio and pretending to be Borut answering my calls to the *Cielito Lindo*. The evening is capped off by a happy reunion with the rest of the team. Apparently the mood out there was extremely tense, and I'm reluctant to reveal to them while they were stranded for twenty-four hours, we were lounging around in a five-star hotel. Instead, I try to empathize by describing the horrors of our evening and the unbearable waiting and worrying we were forced to endure. Martin is well-rested and intends to swim to Iquitos as quickly as possible.

February 6—Tatshitea, Peru

A rapidly rising globe of crimson greets a robust and well-rested Martin Strel, who awakens early to stroke his way out of the bustling city of Pucallpa and back into the outer fringes of civilization. Unfortunately, last-second repairs on the support boat become an all day affair, and by noon Martin's small escort boat has again lost radio contact.

Martin needs to blow off some steam, and today his target is Paul Marchand, who'd joined us for the morning to do a little filming for the documentary. He expected to be out for a few hours. With shaved head and pimp hat, the hip world traveler and Hollywood roustabout is quite a contrast to my Wisconsin, tobacco-chewing, flannel-shirt-wearing self, but we fast become friends and are spending a lot of time chatting while Martin swims. Paul shares with me adventurous stories about his vagabonding travels throughout Asia as the long hours of morning quickly tick away.

"Paul, hey Paul, no talking to Matt," the swimmer suddenly stops and booms. "Matt needs eyes on river. Paul, this is not Los Angeles, this is jungle." We figure that while Martin is swimming, we can ventriloquize our conversation through closed lips. I face forward, and keep the whistle in my mouth. We're soon busted again. "No more Paul in the boat with Matt. Never again. This is not vacation. This is not Hollywood. No more." He doesn't wait for a response, just says what he has to say and continues swimming.

By afternoon, we're out of food and water and looking for a safe place to wait for the rest of the team and discover something to eat. Suddenly, a jubilant Martin comes out of a heap of floating sticks with a beautiful papaya he finds suspended in the Amazonian debris. We have a little papaya cutting ceremony on the hull of the boat, and although we offer to give Martin a portion of our share, he insists that we need to eat something as well. Unfortunately, the damn thing is completely raw and tastes like chalk. We remain hungry and Martin is grumpy again.

A Peruvian Coast Guard boat from Pucallpa comes to inform us of some problems with pirates between here and Contamana, and to request we don't continue without the safety of the large support boat. We hungrily watch them wolf down their MRI lunches as they idle beside us. I ask them to pass a message to Borut on the *Cielito Lindo* that we'll be waiting for them at the village of Tacshitea.

By late afternoon, a village with at least ten huts appears on the right shore. According to our unreliable map, we've reached Tacshitea, a smiling little Venetian community consisting of roughly sixty people and thirty canoes. Amazonian canoes are basically nothing more than trees that have been dug out in the middle to hold people yet stay afloat.

We're very hungry and when we ask a man on a floating store for food, he sends his little boy, Manuel, in a small dugout canoe to get a chicken. Later Manuel tells me that it makes him sad to hear the chicken cry as he holds it before his sister comes to kill it. He also tells me that he has eight brothers and sisters, and three who had died. We look around for a beer during our four-hour wait, but there are no refrigerators to be found and the only option is hot cerveza.

When Paul announces he's done eating and goes to use the bathroom, which is actually just a tiny room with a plank missing from the floor for a pee hole, Martin is shocked to see that

Paul has left some fairly large chicken scraps stuck to a few of the bones. "Paul said he was hungry!" he leans over the table to tell me in shocked disbelief. Grabbing Paul's plate, he scrapes off one of the partially eaten bones to me and takes the other two for himself. I've had enough to eat also, but know better than to leave food when Martin is watching.

We try to sleep on a rickety wooden platform while we wait for the *Cielito Lindo*, but the mosquitoes are relentless, so we strap on headlamps, jump back into the escort boat and head upstream. We meet them five miles up from the little village.

This is the third consecutive day Martin has been frustrated by boat problems. How can Martin Strel make it down the Amazon while our boat can't even seem to survive?

The lead guide on the boat, Alfredo Chavez, has been taking a lot of heat from the Strels. I personally like the guy a lot; he just doesn't concern himself with the North American concept of time. We've learned to triple all estimates of his as to when something will be completed. For instance, if a gas stop is scheduled to take a half hour, we plan for an hour and a half. Alfredo finds me snoozing at the keyboard late tonight and advises me there are only three things that are important in life: health, love, and time, or lack thereof. Then he adds a fourth, money, which discounts the admiration I'd just gained for him. Later on I discover two more of his "most important things:" whisky and ayahuasca, the latter being a strong psychedelic brew made from jungle vines.

February 7—Santa Ana, Peru

Martin finally has a day that allows him to swim at his full potential from dawn until dusk without waiting for the support boat. A determined Martin swims seventy-four miles today, even though an uncommon three-day drought has dropped the river a few feet and slacked off the current slightly. There are fewer whirlpools and debris to impede his progress, and we don't have to blow the whistles as often. The river is still subsiding from the biggest flood to hit the upper Amazon in a hundred years. As a result, the current is much faster than we projected and we're two full days ahead of schedule.

After breaststroking for three hours or so, Martin usually gives his shoulder a break by rolling onto his back and kicking for awhile. He has a little ritual in which he'll pick up a stick and examine it, then break it into pieces and throw the pieces away, all the while still swimming on his back. Sometimes he'll take an especially long stick and hold it up like an antenna and say something like, "Matt, look this," then laugh.

Another of Martin's tricks is telling himself stories in his head while swimming. Often we'll hear a strange gurgling noise as he laughs underwater. Martin once told me that he can only swim when he stops thinking about swimming. Some days, he's halfway through a story when it gets dark, and he wants to keep going so he can get to the ending.

Personally, I think calling it "telling himself stories" cheapens what's really occurring in Martin's mind. Martin gives day dreaming a whole new definition. He can spend ten hours swimming only two meters from my face, and be completely oblivious to my presence. Or his own for that matter. He's really not even there.

He's somewhere else, deep in the archives of his mind, yet the arms and legs of the greatest marathon swimmer in the world just keep moving forward.

Actually, the world's greatest distance swimmer was not always a swimmer. Martin was a competitive gymnast in high school. Borut once showed me a black and white photo of a lean, fifteen-year-old Martin, with bulging muscles and a mischievous grin. He could do hundreds of pushups without tiring and walk on his hands for a hundred meters. His gymnastics career abruptly ended when he disobeyed his father to peddle away on his bicycle thirty-five miles to attend a gymnastics meet in nearby Ljubljana. His father needed him at home to tend to the chickens, and was so upset over Martin even asking to get out of his chores to attend the competition that he beat him soundly and forbade him from future competitions. Martin's coach told him not to worry. He patted Martin on the shoulder and explained to the young man that he was a natural-born swimmer, not a gymnast.

I can't help but try to imagine what was going through Martin's mind when he got on that bicycle and rode thirty-five miles one way to attend the meet. I bet it was a great feeling for him to finally take a stand against the man who'd been so hard on him. Thirty-five miles is a long way for a fifteen-year-old boy.

Near dusk, the *Cielito Lindo* pulls up to the small village of Santa Ana to dock for the night. A handful of curious people begin to gather on a hill along the waterfront. As the sunburned and exhausted swimmer touches the shoreline and walks up the bank, a wave of fear creeps across the ensemble. Women and children frantically run for their huts and a group of men gather to confer.

The village chief politely asks our Peruvian captain to find a different place to anchor. An old shaman had prophesized that demons would come on a boat from the mountains. We find refuge across the river at Suspiro.

February 8—Inahuaya, Peru

"Ha, maybe you need to sleep for another half hour," a perceptive Martin jokes with me as I show up five minutes late for the 5:30 team breakfast. Jamie, John and I were drinking seventy-cent-a-bottle cane whisky when he retired for the night. The more dangerous the trip gets, the more momentary we all become. Songs sound better, foods taste better, and seventy-cent-a-bottle cane whisky is fun to drink.

Martin swims strongly again today. He stops long enough to have a drink, eat another floating papaya, and tell us the story of his first swimming victory, at the age of ten. Some soldiers happened to walk by the creek he'd dammed near his hometown of Mokronog and thought it would be a nice day to take a dip. The group decided to have a race from one side of the small lake to the other, with the winner receiving a bag of beer. A ten-year-old Martin was able to out-swim the entire group of grown men, and soon realized he could make bets with other men in order to help provide his poor family with sustenance and impress his father. All he could think while swimming was how proud his father would be if he were to run into the house triumphantly with the bag of beer.

I can't help but imagine that in Martin's mind, there is no one left to compete against. Now he competes against himself and against Mother Nature.

Martin cranks out another tiresome seventy-two miles, stopping long enough at Contamana to wolf down a huge lunch while the crew loads the boat with crate after crate of beer, wine, and food. A huge throng of people is waiting on a pedestrian bridge near the port to watch him swim into town.

Martin is swimming through an area with a recent history of pirate activity and a reputation as a narco-trafficking hub. Dr. de Leonni Stanonik has been ambitious after the incident where the boat lost control upstream of Pucallpa and she tearfully warned those aboard the damaged boat, "We're all going to die." She's contacted the president of Peru, Alan Garcia, and arranged for the employment of a military escort boat and two soldiers to stay on the ship with us at all times. I can't see this lasting long, mostly because of sleeping and eating logistics. Martin has only one brief comment about the matter, "More people, more problems."

The addition of the soldiers is causing some contention amongst the Peruvian crew members. They say, "If the men with guns tell us to do something, we're forced to do it."

Questions are also arising as to who will feed these men and where will they sleep. Paul tells me that it's more dangerous to have a military presence then to be without one, partially due to remnants of the Sendero Luminoso, a group of guerilla rebels from the late eighties and early nineties who targeted Peruvian soldiers. Now I'm afraid to go in the boat wearing my camo raingear.

Hundreds of curious children wait patiently outside our docked boat in hopes to catch a glimpse of the swimmer at the charming little village of Inahuaya. The horde grows as Martin boards a taxi to take him the half-mile or so to the town. I try to keep up with the fastest boys in the village at the front of the pack following the taxi until jungle heat and thirst makes me slow down to a walk. The boys all stop running to wait for me.

The mayor directs Martin, Jamie, and me into a small auditorium, where we sit on a stage on display for the two hundred or so onlookers. There is no real ceremony, just us sitting and all the people gawking at us. Valter Stepan, a Slovenian day trader who'd signed on to be an assistant cook and helper for the expedition, keeps a large group of children occupied by taking their picture with his digital camera, then showing each child their own face zoomed in. Valter is one of the most peaceful and gentle men I've ever encountered, and although he joined us without a clearly defined role, he's been busy doing any little thing possible to help make the expedition run smoothly. Having never seen a digital camera, the children are laughing so loudly at Valter's pictures that nobody can even hear the unamplified ramblings of Alfredo as he describes Martin's swim.

Martin sits in a pool of sweat, peacefully nodding and smiling occasionally, while most of the adults try to get the children to be quiet. Jamie and I just sit there feeling uncomfortable as three women in the front row breastfeed their babies within ten feet of our raised platform, while Alfredo keeps talking, even though nobody can hear him.

After twenty minutes, a soaking-wet Martin can take no more of the heat in the crowded, disorganized auditorium. We have a big scare when Martin takes a nasty spill on a small muddy hill, but after a few uncertain moments he appears to be all right, albeit a little dirty. A sprained ankle could put the entire expedition in jeopardy.

Much of the team takes advantage of being anchored at the town to have some beers and talk to some young ladies. We always try to anchor near a settlement of some kind, but usually the villages aren't big enough to have a bar. Apparently, anchoring near the largest habitation possible is a safety precaution as pirates are less likely to attempt to rob a boat near a place where help can be obtained.

February 9—Puerto Grau, Peru

Martin takes a break from swimming this morning to have a drink and tell us a story of when he was learning English in Ljubljana. After the lesson, his teacher invited him out for a beer in a bar known to be a hangout for Serbians. One beer led to another, until the teacher was pickled and declaring in a voice that was a little too loud, "To hell with all Serbs. All Serbs should be killed." Martin noticed that many eyes were on them, and quickly convinced the man to discreetly leave the bar before they both got shot. For the next few months, men from the bar would ask him where his friend was and when he might be coming back to visit them.

We look forward to these breaks of Martin's. In the rare instances in which he does open up to us, he usually has something profound to say, either deadly serious or deeply amusing. Sometimes I'll watch him and think he's about to come up and talk, only to have him continue swimming for several more hours in silence. It's painful to see him swim hour after hour, day after day, sometimes without stopping for even a drink for three hours. At times I'm convinced he's not even real, then he'll suddenly stop swimming, pop his head out of the water, stare off into the sky distantly, and reveal something shockingly personal about himself, convincing me that he really is human.

I'm astonished at his torrid pace, averaging about sixty-two miles a day. Amazingly, his World Record for continuous swimming is 313 miles over the course of 84 hours in the cold, flooded waters of the Danube. Of all Martin's swimming records, I find this one to be the most difficult to comprehend.

Physical deterioration is a reality today for the first time on the expedition. Painful blisters are growing wherever Martin's flippers make contact with his skin. To make matters worse, he's developed an irritating rash on both feet as an allergic reaction of sorts is occurring between his skin and the rubber from the flippers. His sunburn is becoming more severe. We haven't had rain now for five days.

While Martin is swimming near the eddy line off a large point, we see a large commotion on the surface of the water. A feeding frenzy occurs as several small fish appear to be feeding on something large and already dead. The swift current carries us several hundred meters past the spot before we can even notify Martin or figure out exactly what it is.

What is Martin's biggest fear? The piranha? The candirú? It's a snake, but not the anaconda. The creature that Martin fears most is the Bushmaster snake. "One touch from the Bushmaster and you'll be dead in twenty minutes," Martin warns the team as we dock for the evening along a grassy bank at the sporty little village of Puerto Grau. He has forbidden us from walking in the jungle at night. "If you leave the boat after dark you may never come back." This nocturnal predator is known for its long fangs and can reach lengths up to fourteen feet. The Latin term for the Bushmaster means, "brings silent death." Entering the river in the early morning and exiting at dusk will be the most dangerous time for Martin. Snakes also occasionally hitch rides on floating debris. Although the Bushmaster isn't prevalent near here, it will be a constant concern as we move farther downstream into its natural habitat.

February 10—Saman, Peru

After another sweaty night swatting away at mosquitoes, Martin reenters the river, energized by a quick breakfast of scrambled eggs and coffee. The sun is relentless, and he's baked for the sixth consecutive day without rain. This is the wet season in the rainforest, and we were told to expect some heavy downpours at least once a day. It showered every day back in Atalaya. The whole crew is hoping for some precipitation to ease Martin's pain.

Martin's weight loss is beginning to concern us. He has dropped fifteen pounds in nine days, way ahead of the pace from previous expeditions. The problem is that he sweats all day in the river, and then sweats all night killing bugs in his stuffy cabin. "Three days of rain and I'll be a new man," he reassures us. Although he's starting to show the first signs of wearing down, we celebrate Martin's 1,000th kilometer late this morning.

Three dolphins swim beside Martin and vocalize regularly for six miles. John teases Martin at lunch by telling him that dolphins regularly mistake swimmers for other dolphins and may be considering him as a potential mate. Later, I find out that there is some truth to this, as swimmers have been injured by accident as curious dolphins nose up for a closer investigation.

The jungle seems to be getting wilder as we near the equator. Its multi-green masses of foliage and Tarzan vines are alive with sound, yet we rarely are able to see the source of that sound. I feel the eyes upon us, not just of the animals, but of people as we pass their dwellings without even knowing it. We often see canoes camouflaged up into the high grasses and sometimes I can just make out the shape of a little hut tucked away in the thick jungle greenery. I know there are people back there somewhere, but rarely do we glimpse them. They hide when we go by, but I know they can see us just fine.

We go down a narrow chute before dark that reveals all sorts of colorful birds who squawk their own variously unique forms of jungle music. Our guides can tell each bird by the sound it makes, but I can never seem to get the pronunciation down and soon give up trying. Martin is fearful of reptiles when swimming close to shore, and I am reprimanded for taking pictures of birds and dolphins and not watching ahead of him for dangerous predators.

Blister problems are continuing to pain Martin, and he surprises us by stopping a full hour before sunset today. I guess he must have completed a long story in his mind and didn't want to get started on another one only to have to interrupt it. He still was able to muscle his way to sixty-seven miles. Martin very rarely stops before sunset, and usually swims way too late, forcing us to scramble for a place to anchor in the dark. The sun is nearly straight overhead here near the equator, and as a result, takes a more direct line down when setting. Up North, I have a trick where I extend a hand and count the fingers until sunset, each finger representing fifteen minutes. That doesn't work here. When the sun sets down here, it nose-dives, signaling to millions of hungry mosquitoes the time to come out and feast on us. We've been told that we're now entering the malaria zone.

The nightlife in Saman is interesting. We enter a boarded barn with peeling green paint for an old fashioned ho-down. A bucket of some kind of alcoholic mix sits in the middle of the twenty guys and two girls who sit around the perimeter of the huge room on shabby benches. One drunken man with a plastic glass makes his rounds offering half cups of the mystery drink. As our buzzes are setting in, the rain starts. Buckets of rain turn everything in town into mud. After we run out of drinks, I am nominated to go with Jarvez and the soldiers to get more. Ever since the night in Pucallpa, I've noticed Jarvez watches out for me whenever we go exploring in little jungle towns.

We walk through a tunnel of darkness, my only indication of direction being Jarvez' shoes slopping through the mud. At one point we come dangerously close to the river. I hope desperately the world will not give way beneath my feet, and wish I was back on the boat. An old song from Blind Faith enters into my head: "and I'm wasted and I can't find my way home."

February 11—Victoria, Peru

Martin has acquired some sort of stomach complication. He's not one to admit illness, but for those of us who know him, it's obvious when he's ill. He spends more time on his back, rarely talks, and never drinks anything when we offer it to him. Back on the Mississippi in 2002, he became so ill that he'd lose consciousness while kicking and bouncing back and forth between our kayaks for minutes at a time. We'd pad his head with the palms of our hands to lessen the impact and redirect him to the other side. Occasionally, we'd smell something and notice a cloud of brown trailing him in the water. At the end of each day we'd lift him out of the water, carry him to the van, he'd pass out, we'd carry him to his hotel bed, and his daughter, Nina, would feed him soup by hand. Then he'd get up the next day and do it all over again.

"How do you feel?" I ask him during lunch.

"I'm terrible," he returns. Stomach problems and parasites scare me more than anacondas and piranhas. I'm not sure what bugs are dangerous, but we all have little blood dots on our forearms and ankles. The thought of being impregnated with some sort of little worm that will cause problems for us up to years in the future is sobering.

Martin isn't the only one who isn't feeling well. Half the crew has been experiencing stomach problems over the last two weeks, and I blame it on the presence of the buckets of blood. The stuff is completely rancid from being out in the hot sun for so many days and although it's kept covered, the putrid smell still escapes, especially when the wind is right. It must be filled with all sorts of nasty bacteria. Although we know that these are piranha-infested waters, we also know piranhas are only reputed to hit a target that is already bleeding. I recommend to Borut that we ditch the blood completely. We finally compromise on acquiring fresh blood every few weeks and getting rid of the rotten stuff.

We've heard that we should always stay close to our larger support boat. There are small bands of pirates in the area around Tierra Blanco who will rob us if they feel we're an easy mark. We're still in narco territory. In the early afternoon, a boat with three tough looking hombres approaches swiftly. I warn Martin to stay near the boat, and the soldier stands up in ready position. I'm not sure if it's the presence of the soldier or just my paranoia playing with me, but the boat turns sharply and veers off toward a nearby village.

Martin is usually fearless to such situations. When swimming the Danube from source to sea, he was warned to bypass an area known for being inhabited by some dangerous gypsies. Rather than follow the advice, he instead found a small snake, put it into his mouth, and swam to shore with the live serpent squirming to free itself. The feared gypsies were in awe, backed off like they'd seen a ghost, and he instantly won their respect and adoration.

Near dusk, a small pink dolphin surfaces within five yards of Martin. "Look, dolphin," the backstroking swimmer exclaims, pointing behind us like a little kid. He's been in a very quiet mood over his last few days of illness, and it's nice to see the dolphin cheer him up a bit.

Dinner is pretty quiet. When Martin is in a foul mood, we all tend to give him plenty of space. When someone asks him if he's feeling sick, he responds "We're all a little sick here. Now just God can help us." I'm not sure if he's joking or not, but his cynical half laugh gives me a chill, especially considering that he'd only uttered about ten words all day. Amazingly, he was able to cover sixty-five miles. It's the lowest total he's had in days, but awesome nonetheless.

February 12—San Carlos, Peru

Martin stops swimming to ask me how many kilometers until the next village. He's tired and wants to have an early lunch. I tell him we've left the main channel of the Ucayali and are on a side chute called the Puinahua Canal, thus we have no maps for the next few days. "I don't believe you," he says. I defend myself, challenging him to bet me ten Peruvian sol. "Show me map and GPS," he grunts.

Martin swims near the boat and I hang our map over the side, showing him that our GPS coordinates are off the charts. He begins to swear in Slovene while I consider the slim possibilities of collecting on the wager. At least I can guess he's feeling better than yesterday. The more he yells at us, the better he feels; his silence is usually a red flag.

Martin is like a big diesel truck. He's the most powerful thing on the road, but occasionally he's got to blow out a big puff of black smoke. Those of us who know Martin realize that he has to keep a jacked-up mentality in order to maintain the energy needed for such a swim, and it's necessary for him to release some exhaust fumes from time to time. I expect Martin to yell at me, and I don't take it personally when he does. It's part of the swim, but some people have a hard time accepting this.

He spends a few hours on his back today, giving his shoulders a little bit of needed rest. Just after having a drink, he finds a stick shaped like a small cane, picks it up, and spends the next two hours silently examining it and kicking along, lost in some sort of cane-wielding day dream.

A troop of howler monkeys brings us all out of the slumber. They're small, elusive creatures, but their howling sounds like a windstorm that can be heard miles away on a calm day. Occasionally we'll turn a corner and surprise them, watching them swing through the trees and vines into safety, but usually they disappear before we get a chance to see them.

The Amazon is teeming with wildlife, but it doesn't just jump out at you like it does in the movies. Things here are camouflaged and subtle. Closer inspection of an area thought to be bare often reveals myriad species, all trying not to attract attention to themselves so as not to become the meal of a larger predator. The predators are quite stealthy too. We may pass within meters of a stalking jaguar on the shoreline, look right at it and not know it there. Occasionally we turn off the motors for an hour or so and paddle alongside the swimmer, soaking in the symphony of the jungle.

Martin starts talking again in the afternoon. This is a very good sign. He's using the vision for his next swim as a distraction to eat miles on this one. His explorer friend, Will Steger, has been telling him stories of the Yukon River. It appeals to Martin because it's very swift and has no dams. The Yukon is coincidentally my last paddling dream. Martin and I spend the final few hours of the day planning logistics for the trip, including dropping off foodstuffs, bear precautions, water temperature concerns, and raft/kayak escort boat plans. I tell him stories about grizzly encounters my fiancée Kristina and I had last summer while backcountry hiking in Denali, and he's excited and full of questions about bear and moose behavior. Alaska is one of the final places Martin has yet to visit. He's been to 140 countries but has never experienced the harsh wilderness of the last great frontier.

Martin took a long lunch and even quit a little early tonight. His fifty-seven miles would seem huge on any other expedition, but considering the fact he topped sixty-two on every other full day of swimming, we're a tad concerned about the drop.

February 13—Requena, Peru

We have another silent breakfast as Martin is still feeling ill. He still won't admit he has diarrhea. It's so early in the trip and Martin is already so shredded, I can't seem to imagine him swimming another 2,500-plus miles. As I watch him swim, somewhere in the back of my mind, I'm waiting for that giant splash as some sort of monster from the dark water comes up from the depths to devour him. I'm here to help protect him, yet that subconscious, morbid fascination still lingers in the back of my scalp.

Although a little sick, he takes advantage of the cooler hours of the early morning, quickly passing a family of six in a large canoe. Two of the boys struggle to contain pigs, while their sisters keep charge of the chickens. Hundreds of unripe bananas are strapped to the front of the tipsy craft.

The Peruvians I've seen and met so far seem to marry and have many children very young. They gather what they need from the jungle, and spend the afternoons lost in sport and leisure. They look at us with a sort of dull interest, as if wondering what the gringos are doing, yet shyly mind their own business. They find us amusing, especially the hair on our arms and face and the way we talk. They gaze on us as if we are incompetent to face the challenges of the terrain, yet are quick to offer assistance, for a few sol, of course.

Martin reminds the team at lunch to take our malaria pills regularly as we're now entering an area with more active carriers of the epidemic. The pills themselves can cause one to feel pretty crappy. Side effects range from nausea, vomiting, and diarrhea, to visual disturbances, strange dreams, and hair loss. The mosquitoes are a nuisance here, and none of us go outside at night without 100 percent DEET. A mosquito that takes Martin's blood could probably swim from here to Europe without resting.

Malaria is just one insect problem the team needs to consider. Small flies can impregnate our skin with microscopic eggs that might not hatch until we get home. Stomach parasites find a permanent home in virtually all those who live here, and some of us may be unaware of other exotic souvenirs for years.

We've been in the Puinahua Canal now for three days, and Martin isn't happy. He constantly asks questions we can't answer, because we don't have any maps for this portion of river. "How many kilometers to Iquitos? How many kilometers to Requena? How far to the next village?" When Jamie or I remind him we have no way of knowing, he laughs at us condescendingly, swears in Slovene, shakes his head, and continues swimming.

Another relentless day of sun has baked Martin's lips into a crusty, oozing mess. He's in the habit of swimming on his back wearing the doctor's floppy ladies hat during the peak hours of sun. Twice per day she cakes on a thick layer of white protective surfer lotion around his mouth like a clown, and those of us on the escort boat are having a really hard time looking at him without breaking into tearful laughter. He knows he looks goofy, but this is the best solar protection he can get.

Coming out of a narrow slough near an island, we witness a feeding frenzy as negro dolphins corral a school of baitfish. They're smaller than the pink dolphins, and don't follow as close to the boat. The pinks are with us every day and we no longer get excited and scramble for our digital cameras to attempt to capture the elusive targets at every sighting. I already have dozens of confusing pictures of open water as they resubmerge the moment I open the shutter.

Martin tries to make Requena, but comes up about seven miles short, finishing the day at sixty-eight miles. The support boat has gone ahead to resupply our water and beer. Martin is frustrated with Peruvian wine. During our expedition on the Paraná in Argentina, a bottle of wine cost the equivalent of about a dollar. Here, it runs about eight dollars. Martin enjoys a glass of wine now and then, but has decided to do without it from now until we reach Brazil. Instead, he'll have to just be content with an occasional beer.

February 14—Capitan Clavero, Peru

"Martin, do you feel better this morning?" I ask.

"I'm 70 percent. I don't know what's wrong," he answers. For the only time other than when I saw him suck back tears at Mile Zero of the Mississippi, I detect a small quiver in his always-confident tone. Martin lost an unprecedented five pounds yesterday, and has now shed twenty-two pounds in thirteen days. For a moment, I think of Barry Bonds. He's old, still great, but how long can he last? Martin is fifty-two years old and is covering over sixty-two miles a day. How many could he do on this fast river if he was in his prime?

Martin was very slender until he joined the Yugoslavian army for his mandatory sixteen-month tour of duty at the age of twenty-six. It was here that he discovered the pleasures of beer drinking, and the excess tended to accumulate in his belly. As he grew older, his taste matured, and he became fond of Slovenian Cvicek wine. Although he was packing on the pounds as he grew older, marathon swimming is entirely different from sprint swimming. A man slowly deteriorates over the course of a multiweek swim. The bigger Martin is at the beginning of a swim, the more cushion he has to withstand the pounding.

The weight loss is a much bigger drop than previous expeditions, however; never has Martin been forced to endure such heat and direct sun for so many continuous days. The heat and humidity is wreaking havoc on our bodies. Everyone on the team is always exhausted, but while we're sleeping, Martin is still swimming.

He's like a machine. He just swims and swims and swims in the same methodical rhythm, then stops once every three hours to say maybe two words or ask for a kilometer count. My job is to blow a whistle whenever any danger is eminent, but it's easy to get lost in a daydream and then get yelled at after Martin bangs his face on a floating log.

Today, I find myself daydreaming about home, and all the fat people back in the States: For all of you who'd like to lose weight fast, we have the perfect club for you to join. All you have to do is swim the Amazon River. We guarantee you'll lose twenty pounds in the first two weeks or die trying.

One of the soldiers on board the boat is visibly ill today. He's passed out in the back of the boat, and he's gotten up twice to heave overboard. His constant wheezing and snot-dripping is a huge point of concern for Martin, who is scared to death of acquiring influenza. He orders the soldier out of the mess hall and to stay away from the rest of the team until he feels better. Some of the Peruvians are very offended by this.

Martin admits his diarrhea for the first time today. He demands to know if Jamie and I have been rinsing his drink containers with Amazon water. We show him step-by-step how we go to the hot water tank for the daily ritual. Martin has only been drinking approximately two pints of his hydration drink per day, compared to the eight we prepare for him. He still has a beer with lunch and dinner. This lack of proper hydration and insistence on ingesting diuretics is perplexing to all of us, but we can't convince him otherwise. He somehow thinks that part of the problem is because of the lack of his normal regiment of light red wine, something he refers to as a secret among top European athletes.

Martin fights his way through another sixty-seven miles today. Sixty-seven miles sounds like an unfathomable amount, but with Martin, it's all about hours in the water. If he's in the water eleven hours, he's going to cover about six miles per hour with this strong current, sick or not sick. How does he turn off the pain and kick through the fatigue? I know that when I have a case of the runs, I don't get off the couch if I can help it. I don't understand how the body of a fifty-two year-old can take such abuse. At dinner, his drooping eyes and obvious exhaustion betray him; he looks his age and then some.

February 15—Ocho de Mayo, Peru

Today is a major milestone as Martin negotiates dangerous whirlpools at the confluence of the Ucayali and Maranon Rivers, considered by most as the start of the Amazon River proper. The Ucayali drains the Peruvian Andes, while the Ecuadorian Amazon flows through the Maranon. Further upstream, the Amazon is known by different names as we've spent the last fifteen days on the Rio Tambo, Rio Ucayali, and Puinahua canal. We only have two months and approximately 2,500 miles to go. Yippee.

As if the confluence isn't dangerous enough, the film crew doesn't get the shot they need, and Martin is toted back upstream to shoot the footage again. He's not happy about this, nor is Borut. An eerily similar confluence on the Yangtze had sucked Martin underwater for thirty seconds.

A new member joins the film crew today, Chris Maxwell from Joshua Tree, California. Known as "the specialist," the blonde, 22-year-old, 115-pounder is reputed to be a young genius with an uncanny ability to solve myriad problems. He likes to talk about lucid dreaming and astral projection, and has already sparked a new energy into the twenty-two other souls onboard the boat.

The crew lunches on wild alligator today. Late last night, a four-foot Lagarto was found slumbering near the anchor rope, and was quickly disposed of by a few of the Peruvians and a large stick.

Every day we devise new ways to help Martin combat the sun. Today, we strap a white pillowcase around his head with holes for eyes, nose, and mouth. He complements this scary-looking mask with an oversized ladies floppy hat. We thought yesterday was tough with the clown-paint, but today it's impossible to look at him with a straight face. A big group of people paddles by in a canoe loaded with bananas. When they see the swimming phantom, a little girl onboard begins to cry and they quickly paddle away.

Since we've hit the Amazon proper, the river is nearly twice as wide. Navigation is difficult as there are many islands and more eddies. It's very challenging to find the best current. Martin lets us have it whenever he feels we've made a bad choice in guiding him. He tears into Arturo this afternoon for not holding the boat in a straight line. He makes a fishtailing motion with his arm, then cups both hands, extended them skyward and cries out, "Oh whoa, God help us."

Swimming with the mask is frustrating for Martin. It's hard for him to breathe and very hot. By the end of the day, the area around his mouth is brown with dirt that accumulates from the waves breaking on his face. His lips are blistered and constantly bleeding, and scabs are forming on his nose and upper cheeks. In addition, his eyes are sore and swollen, probably from suntan lotion getting inside his goggles.

An exhausted swimmer lands at the small town of Ocho de Mayo at sunset, covering sixty-two miles on the day. Some ladies offer us some sort of mashed potato–like dish they stir with a big wooden spoon in a huge bowl, using their own spit to help it reach the proper consistency.

February 16—Iquitos, Peru

The Peruvians on board have been buzzing about Iquitos for over a week. Iquitos. Iquitos. Iquitos. We've been hearing the word uttered amongst the men with longing smiles several times a day. We hear a lot of talk about chicas and señoritas and some of these single (and not-single) Peruvian guys look at the arrival into town with hopeful expectation after a long and lonely trip on a boat full of men. All the talk about Iquitos has the gringos fired up too. We need beer, laundry, and Internet access. The thought of seeing a few pretty girls isn't unappealing either.

After a seemingly endless swim through a long slow canal, Martin enters the biggest city in the world that isn't connected to anywhere by road: the famous jungle capital of Iquitos. Iquitos was famous as a prosperous hub during the rubber boom but later suffered as the seeds were smuggled out of the area and rubber farms were set up overseas.

We watch as men pull pigs off a big boat, tie the pigs' legs together, and load the squealing animals three at a time onto motorbike taxis. They treat the live animals like bags of grain, dragging the heavy ones across the concrete, swinging them aboard the vehicles, and strapping them down for the ride.

The entire port is stacked with boats of all sizes, each of them filled with people sleeping. There is no such thing as privacy. Talking with Borut, I look down to see a family of five, all sleeping in a large dugout canoe, only three yards away, directly below us. I'm embarrassed to disturb them, but the entire port is abuzz with the clanging of people loading and unloading cargo all evening, so I figure they're used to it.

A glassy-eyed Valter shows up at 4:30 AM after attending an ayahuasca ceremony with Alfredo. We'd all been invited to partake, but Valter was the only one to accept. Alfredo tells us that the experience was stronger than he anticipated.

The ceremony began with the drinking of a few tablespoons of a liquid. Then the shaman started to sing. After about five minutes the effect began. Visual hallucinations, a feeling of warmth and peace spreading to the body's extremities, and a swimming of the mind. The shaman acted as a guide as future life experiences flashed through Valter's mind like a movie. It's said that ayahuasca is used to both predict the future and as a diagnostic tool. We'd been told by the natives that it's good to use once a year, but not more. Alfredo tells us, "I do it all the time."

February 17—Near Rio Napo Confluence

Some of the crew takes advantage of the stopover at Iquitos to do a little partying. The faces of those around the breakfast table and the lack of presence by others tells a bit of the story. John convinces Martin to wait until 11:30 to leave so his film crew can rent a plane for some aerial shots. The doctor is still trying to acquire satellite equipment, and the supply boat needs a little work. Martin isn't happy to postpone the start, but agrees.

We leave Iquitos as the *Cielito Lindo* is being serviced, hoping to see her again by midafternoon. The river has nearly tripled in size since Atalaya, resulting in difficult navigation through mazes of islands. Wind and waves provide a new obstacle to swimming on the bigger water. Martin swims out of the port of Iquitos with two-foot waves breaking into his face. The current is fast, but the river is huge and windswept, and the channel is difficult to find. Sometimes we can average eight miles an hour, but suddenly the current is gone, and we're doing four, and Martin is looking around and wondering why the progress has been slowed.

We're joined today by Swiss photojournalist, Corrado Filipponi. He's a river veteran who, like Jamie, has paddled the Danube and Mississippi Rivers, but has joined us on this trip to document the photographic aspects of the expedition and translate my website news into German. He also teamed up with Jamie and American guide David Hale to help guide Martin down the Yangtze River in 2004. Combined with my two trips down the Mississippi and the Paraná expedition I joined Martin on in 2003, the three of us have over twenty thousand miles of big river paddling experience.

By dusk, the *Cielito Lindo* has caught up to us and the wind has nearly diminished. We finish the day thirty-nine miles downstream from town.

After dinner, Martin tears into Jamie and me for going to town instead of staying on the boat and guarding the equipment.

"One piece is worth fifty thousand dollars. Believe me, you've never seen this much money. Matt's house isn't worth this much." The two of us, like everyone else on board, had jumped on the first opportunity in weeks to find Internet access and supplies. Personally, I needed whisky and diarrhea medicine. Apparently, Martin had found himself alone on the boat and had reason to vent.

February 18—Pevas, Peru

Martin yells for Jamie to employ the buckets of blood; he screams that he felt something bump into his leg and then something tear into it. In the pandemonium, Jamie throws the blood on the same side of the boat as Martin. Martin frantically circles around to the other side to avoid the blood in the water; he says he was hit three more times before he could get onboard.

Martin is furious at Jamie, and lets him have it the frightening way only Martin can do. He shows us the tears in his wetsuit. Jamie takes the incident hard.

Later Martin suddenly unleashes a tirade of Slovenian swear-words toward Jamie, after two hours of silent swimming, when he looks up from his swimming to notice his cabin door was ajar on the third deck of the *Cielito Lindo*.

The team is in disagreement over the morning incident. Martin is positive he was attacked by piranhas, while Jamie and I both think that he was temporarily hung up on some underwater obstruction like a submerged tree limb or some cable or debris from a sunken boat. Everything I've read about piranhas claims they don't like current and won't attack a swimmer who isn't bleeding, but who knows?

We see a pack of a small monkeys leaping from the end of a small branch to another tree to escape our presence. Martin tells us a story of a right-of-passage he had to go through back in his hometown of Mokronog, in prewar Yugoslavia. The older boys of the village convinced him to climb to the top of a slender pine tree. They tossed him a rope and proceeded to pull him and the top of the tree down at a right angle. When they released the rope he whiplashed back and forth, grasping onto the tree for life until the motion finally subsided.

He often tells us such stories of his youth. Martin grew up in an area where gaining the respect of the other boys meant fighting. After several bloody scraps at the hands of larger youth, he quickly developed the reputation as a tough young brawler that was not to be messed with. Sometimes the schoolmasters themselves would get rough with the boys, and Martin tells us he taught the teachers a thing or two as well.

Alfredo tells us the locals have started a nickname for Martin. They call him, "El Hombre Paiche." The official name of the Paiche is Arapaima Gigas. At fourteen feet long, it's considered the largest freshwater fish in the world.

So why do we follow Martin down the Mississippi, the Danube, the Amazon, or the Yangtze? The answer is simple:

An expedition is 95 percent misery and 5 percent ecstasy. After three weeks of constant motion in a land far away from home, something strange occurs in the soul of a man. He gets broken. The first symptom is a tired or sick feeling, maybe even some fear and a little helplessness. Loneliness. Then something slowly changes within. The old attachments start to fade and he becomes completely present. He forgets about all the crap that keeps him up at night back home. None of it matters anymore.

The same man who may be the shy, passive, no-balls type back home in the office or factory can evolve into a badass who can cause men to quickly look away and ladies to cringe with one glance. He can share a table with the toughest of hombres and throw back beers with unswerving eyes, enjoying every minute of it.

After going home and dealing with all the meaningless details of electricity bills, lawn mowing, mortgage payments, and an unfulfilling job, a period of depression inevitably occurs. Those people back home can't understand why he'd leave his cozy existence behind again for three more months to jump at the next opportunity to subject himself to such misery and danger. But they just don't get it.

February 19—Santa Rita, Peru

Martin attends a sunrise ceremonial dance with indigenous people from the Yagua tribe near Pevas. The ceremony was arranged by Francisco Grippa, a Peruvian artist who Martin met last night at La Casa Del Arte in Pevas. Martin is usually in his room resting by 9:00, but last night, the two carried on like long lost brothers, sharing beers and cheese, exchanging gifts and even swapping shirts.

The Yagua tribe is a peaceful group who wear shredded palm leaves over their privates and red paint on their face. The tribe, originally in the thousands, has seen their population diminish into the hundreds. Not coincidentally, they're one of few indigenous Amazonian tribes to use birth control. Native to the Iquitos area, they have a custom in which the women are the primary breadwinners while the men spend their life pursuing leisure.

Fast currents have aided Martin to a pace of three days ahead of schedule. This is great news for the whole team as we know that when we reach the bigger waters of Brazil, a slower progression can be expected. We still have good current, but it's harder to find. Martin lets us know when we lose it. We carry a speed relaying system with us called "the stupid board." It's one of those kid toys where you can draw a picture using a magnet, then pull a lever to automatically erase. Martin likes us to lean over the side of the boat and show him his speed every fifteen minutes or so. We've learned through the wonders of positive reinforcement that it's good to show him a nice speed of ten, eleven, or twelve. When we get down near six and seven, we're hesitant to show him as he usually stops swimming and demands to know why we've lost the current.

A sunny afternoon is interrupted by a wall of dark clouds. Strong winds kick up out of the Northwest, bringing fierce lightning and sheets of rain. We pull Martin out of the water, just as the wind rips the sun cover off the top of our small boat and knocks the antenna from the top of the *Cielito Lindo*. The team seeks shelter at the small pueblo of Santa Rita. Martin stops swimming early, after covering only fifty-four miles on the day.

Again, I find myself using the words, "only" fifty-four miles. This is similar to the distance of Martin's first world famous swim. Ten years ago he became the first man to ever survive the dangerous crossing from Tunisia, in the continent of Africa, to Pantelleria Island off the coast of Italy. Although not a long distance, fast currents and carnivorous sharks claimed the lives of the other seven men who attempted the swim. I asked him once about the experience, and he told me he was more afraid of the Medusa, or jellyfish, than of the sharks, especially since he wasn't wearing a wetsuit.

Late in the evening, Jamie speaks with me about possibly quitting the expedition at Tabatinga. He feels as if he's become Martin's scapegoat for everything that goes wrong on the expedition. He wants to run it by me before he decides, as I would have to pick up a lot of extra work. I'm not excited to hear the news and try to convince him to stay, but ultimately it's his decision to make.

February 20—Chimbote, Peru

We were awoken in the predawn hours to confusion and the feeling of motion. Someone from the village had cut our anchor rope and the *Cielito Lindo* is now moving. The captain quickly retied the boat in a safe location, but a discussion arose about what had happened. One thought is that some robbers had set us loose in order to get us away from the safety of the village before storming the boat; others surmise that the villagers were unhappy that we were unwilling to share our beer and food and decided to play a mean trick. It's also possible that the feat was done by a drunken prankster. I guess we'll never know.

Because of the strong sun, Martin wears his white mask on particularly sunny days during the midday peak sun hours. The white cloth mask is turning a dirty brown. It's painful to watch his labored breathing as he struggles to get a breath of fresh air through the filthy obstruction. Sometimes he uses one hand to try to pull the sticky cloth away from his face. I ask him if he's having a hard time breathing through the mask. "Yes, but no mask, no protection, no swimming."

The film crew stops for an hour to visit a leper colony near Santa Rosa. Chris tells me he was horrified of the encounter. Someone had told him it was an airborne virus, and as he stood among all the disfigured lepers he figured on about a fifty-fifty chance of contracting the disease.

The pace of the current has noticeably slowed. Martin is grumpy all afternoon as I show him stupid board readings of six, seven, and eight kilometers per hour. Later in the day, we find some fast water and I show him a twelve. "Oh!" he exclaims while nodding his head approvingly. He looks like a grandfather who's been presented a new pair of socks on Christmas day.

A fast current keeps Martin in a good mood all afternoon. When Jamie comes to greet us and help with our gear at the end of the day, Martin starts teasing him. "Jamie, how many beers did you drink today, or maybe you can't remember." Then he looks at me and laughs heartily. "More beers, remember less."

Martin finishes strong, totaling sixty miles on the day. The river has tripled in width and the average current speed has slowed considerably since we left Atalaya. It looks like those days above sixty miles are going to be a thing of the past. Martin has averaged fifty-two miles per day in the last week.

We stop for the night at the town of Chimbote. The Colombian influence is prevalent as we see for the first time men with long black hair and beards. The men from Peru almost exclusively wear their hair short. The town has an army base and a lot of Peruvian soldiers loitering around, making for a very paranoid vibe. Some of the guys from the crew show an interest in a few pretty girls hanging around near the port, but they're very guarded, probably having already been approached each time a new batch of excited young freedom fighters reports to duty.

Martin will be entering Colombian waters tomorrow morning. The team is slightly apprehensive about the reputation of the area as a haven for smuggling operations. Coco paste is made deep in the jungles of Peru and brought by boat to the Colombian border to be processed into cocaine. We're not sure how much of the area's dangerous reputation is factual, but we plan on being cautious nonetheless.

February 21—Colombia-Peru Border

With Jamie still thinking of leaving the expedition, I take a proactive step at breakfast by asking Valter, who'd been in the habit of riding along in the escort boat every morning to relax and take pictures, if he'd mind being the lead navigator this morning. I'd talked to Martin the last evening, appealing to his frugality by demonstrating the need for more time to work on the book and finding a publisher. "Martin, I can make you more money in the big boat then in the small boat." I'd just sold a two-thousand-word essay to the *London Times* for $1,200, and told him I'd give him half.

Valter is upset with me for putting him on the spot, but if Jamie leaves, we'd need him to help cover his shifts. Valter does a good job on his first day as navigator, but makes one small mistake that takes Martin through a stretch of slow, shallow water. At one point Martin stops swimming to stand up in waist high water and address the escort boat. "Valter the genius has found shallow water half a meter deep in the middle of the Amazon."

At some point in the morning, the captain announces to us that we'd crossed the Colombia border. The left bank going from Peru to Colombia was about as eventful as crossing through a cornfield from Minnesota into Iowa. Throughout the day crew members passed the news along. "We're in Colombia now."

"No? Really? It doesn't look any different."

When I show up early for lunch, Martin gives me the cold shoulder. "Matthew, come back in five minutes. Morning swim team eats before the rest of team." I'd always been Martin's guy in the trenches, sweating it out in the kayak next to him. Now, I'm doing clerical work and he thinks of me differently. Ouch.

I go out in the escort boat after lunch, ask Arturo to kill the motor, grab a paddle and straddle the front of the boat. There is no comparison between listening to the jungle and trying to listen to the jungle over the annoying hum of an idling motor. "Martin, have you seen any monkeys today?"

"Yea, there's twenty-two of them on the *Cielito Lindo* right now." Martin has always shown favoritism to the guys who are out in the elements with him.

When the time comes to quit for the night, we find ourselves in a bit of a predicament. Martin had made plans to stop on the Colombian side, but the Peruvians will have nothing of it. They tell us it's too dangerous to sleep on the Colombian bank, and Arturo tells a story of a mass execution of nineteen drug enforcement workers in this area several years ago.

We receive permission to anchor outside a little hut on the Peruvian side. Two naked little boys with spears run along top of a small cut bank throwing at and missing fish every few minutes.

In the evening, a drowsy Martin comes downstairs for a beer and his eyes light up when he witnesses the piles of sol on the kitchen table as Paul, Jamie, John, Chris and I play our weekly game of Texas Hold 'Em. He inquires about the rules and asks questions about the flop, the turn, and the river. He's especially impressed with the aspect of bluffing in the game that results in one collecting huge piles of coin without the burden of showing cards. Martin laughs out loud when he watches Paul lose all of his coins in an especially big pot.

After his soldier days, Martin had survived for a time playing in dangerous card games in the backrooms of Yugoslavia as a professional gambler. Huge amounts of money were exchanged at these games, and often the men involved were not particularly fond of losing. Martin enjoyed the intensity of the gambling but later picked up his guitar and switched careers again, becoming a music teacher. He still has the Peruvian guitar he bought back in Pucallpa, but has yet to gift us with a song.

February 22—Tabatinga, Brazil

We receive a rock star welcome at the Complejo Turistico de Tabatinga by a mob of Martin Strel fans that'd been following the trip since day one. The mayor brings out his entourage of samba dancers and presents Martin with the key to the city.

I'm happy to have finished our two-day stint along the little finger of Colombia that cuts in along the river between Brazil and Peru. From here it will be Brazil for the rest of the trip. There is no comparison between Brazil and Peru. When you cross the border, everything changes. The colors get brighter, the frowns turn into smiles, and everyone wants to dance. The Brazilian women are like creatures from a different planet, and their aggressive gyrations indicate they may be looking to extend their species.

Actually there is a very odd social problem in Brazil. There are too many women. Nobody knows exactly why, but there is such an abundance of Brazilian women that many have become alpha-females, claiming the male for their sole possession and physically defending their catch against other potential alpha-females. They try to seal the deal early, using two of the things they're best at, dancing and sex.

We say goodbye to the Peruvians aboard the *Cielito Lindo* and move onto the M.S. *Cassiquiari*. It's a rainy, quiet farewell as the Peruvians wait for a big tip that never really materializes. Alfredo breathes a big sigh and tells us, "I didn't want to scare you earlier, but I really didn't think we would survive all the way through Peru. It was a lot more dangerous than I told you it would be. We must have just gotten lucky." No wonder he was stoned the whole time.

At lunchtime, Jamie stands up and announces to the team that he will not be accompanying us into Brazil. We expect a big reaction from Martin, but he just nods his head and says, "Okay

Jamie, big mistake for you." Jamie promptly checks in to a motel in Colombia and is robbed of his cell phone and digital camera that same day.

Borut learns that the exchange rate for Brazilian reais (pronounced hay-ICE) was better in nearby Leticia, Colombia. He insists I go with him for the trade. He had $15,000—150 crisp hundreds in a wad—and would save almost $2,000 at the better rate. Great, we were going into the belly of the cocaine and counterfeit money world with fifteen large wadded up in a fanny pack.

We hire two motorcycle drivers to take us on the seemingly endless two-mile ride. The first two cambio windows do not have nearly enough reais to make the exchange. The motorcycle drivers are getting impatient and already know we're carrying a large sum. What would stop them from driving us out to a remote location, machete-slicing us, taking our cash and leaving us to decompose in the jungle? Only the jaguars and slime molds would know where we were as we transformed into Amazonian soil.

The small, shifty looking man at the second window tells us to wait a few minutes while his friend goes to get the money. He leads us through a doorway, then under two blankets that serve as room dividers. He invites us to sit in a cramped, well-lit room on some plastic lawn chairs. I duck back outside to give the drivers a few bills for their waiting time, gripping my motorcycle helmet tightly the whole time.

After fifteen minutes, a bearded man in his forties comes into the room. He has a small blue case and appears very nervous. A small fan cools the room a little. A cat and mouse game begins over who will pull their money out first. Borut throws the entire sum on the table, 150 $100-bills. How do we know that the money they'll give us is real? How do we know they won't storm the room with guns and take our money and kill us? I don't like the feel of things.

The man soon opens his pack and starts pulling out groups of bills, denominations of fifties and twenties, wrapped in rubber bands labeled with grand totals written in black magic markers on a torn off piece of paper, affixed to the top bill by a small piece of tape.

One man watches as I count the reais, while Borut watches as another man counts the dollars. The fan starts blowing some of the money around, so we turn it off. There are so many piles of twenties that after making sure the first few contained the thousand Brazilian reais as indicated, I begin comparing the height of stacks. With an exchange rate of 2.3 reais to the dollar, we were looking at nearly 35,000 reais in 1,700 20-reais bills. My count comes up about 5,000 reais short. I feel under my chair with a foot to locate my motorcycle helmet, anticipating the worst. Borut is angry at the bearded man, but the bearded man tells us, "tranquilo, tranquilo" ("it's cool, it's cool"). He explains we had cleaned out their stash and they were waiting for more to be delivered. I'm fairly confident they figured we wouldn't notice the difference.

I excuse myself, subtly taking with me one of the twenty notes, cross under the two blankets and out onto the streets. Crossing the street to a nearby market, I purchase two Cokes, just to make sure the money isn't counterfeit. It is okay. I leave the Cokes and a few more bills with the drivers, promising we'll be finished shortly and trying to get a read on them to see if we can trust them to bring us out of Colombia safely.

By the time I get back, Borut has finished the transaction, except for seven of our hundreds which they wouldn't accept. We reboard the bikes and head out of town. Borut's fanny pack could not hold all the stacks of bills, so both of our pockets are stuffed. I instruct my driver to follow Borut at twenty yards so I can watch out for suspicious followers, all the while being careful not to allow any of the stacks to fall out of my pockets and into the streets for some lucky passerby.

The seemingly endless ride back to Brazil goes off without a hitch. We tip the drivers, stash the money on the boat, and clean up for a night of partying in Tabatinga. Chris keeps us entertained all night, jumping on stage with his oversized shades and attempting to dance with the samba dancers while we all sit on the sidelines sipping Skol beer. Martin goes to bed early to prepare to continue swimming tomorrow morning after clearing customs. Brazil has already instilled a refreshing new energy to our weary team.

February 23—Tabatinga, Brazil

We clear customs without a problem, although several disputes arise with the motorcycle taxis, who charge us amounts ranging from three to fifteen reais for the same exact ride. We've found it's best to always come to an agreement on price before getting on the taxi, but some on the team still haven't grasped this concept.

I'm itching to get back on the river as our 11:00 departure time comes and goes without an appearance by Martin. The doctor found him with an irregular heartbeat this morning, apparently as a result of severe dehydration. By early afternoon Martin had consumed four bowls of soup broth and several hydra drinks. He's ready to go.

The first day with a new crew is always a huge challenge. It's nearly impossible to explain to the escort boat driver that he's not there to follow Martin, but to lead him. Martin can't see where he's swimming and depends entirely on the boat for direction. As we leave Tabatinga, Martin starts drifting to his left, so the boat keeps moving farther left in order to get away from the swimmer, and Martin keeps following. I have to deliver several sharp blasts with my safety whistle as we come dangerously close to some moored ships.

Martin is very picky about the proximity of the boat to him. He likes it exactly two meters to his left when doing the crawl, but slightly farther away and behind him when on his back. Also, the time of day and angle of the sun occasionally calls for the boat to switch sides.

We zigzag out of town, and every time I overcome my lack of Portuguese to positively reinforce the driver for the times he does a good job, the camera crew radios us to get out of the shot so they can film Martin with our new Indian princess mascot, a half-naked bombshell of twenty years in a Pocahontas costume straddling the front of a newly acquired media boat. The skimpy thong bikini is a distraction to everyone, and the driver of the media boat keeps cutting us off and I have to wave him away, only to have the film crew yell at me again for blocking their shot of Martin with Pocahontas in the background. My driver is a tough looking hombre with tattooed muscles and a cigarette hanging out of his mouth. He's visibly becoming frustrated with me because he can't understand what I want him to do.

Paul comes onboard the escort boat to do some filming for the first time since Martin tore into him back by Pucallpa. He brings Chris, the specialist, to do sound. While filming a clip of Martin swimming, we somehow convince Chris to jump in the water, telling him he had to be sure to pinch off his groin area with one hand so a candirú can't enter. The results are hysterical as he lasts only twenty seconds of one-handed swimming before needing to be rescued. Even Martin has a laugh at this episode.

After a full month of diarrhea and losing seven pounds from my already skinny frame, I've started Cipro to kill whatever parasite or worm I have crawling around in my belly. The biggest precaution is to stay out of direct sun, hard to do all day in a small boat near the equator.

By late afternoon the sun subsides and some mean looking clouds move in. I radio the *Cassiquiari* to get ready to pick us up, but Martin laughs at me and tells me that it will not rain. I guarantee him it will be raining within half an hour. We never get a drop. Martin's uncanny ability to predict the weather has always impressed me.

The combination of a new crew, the Indian princess distraction, a late start, dehydration, and a slower than expected current results in Martin covering only a disappointing twenty-three miles on the day.

This boat has less of a jungle feel as techies with the live web streaming have their equipment scattered all over the common areas. Although the rooms are terribly cramped and the dining area is open air and thus filled with mosquitoes, we do have huge satellites which provide for wireless Internet access.

As several of us, doused in 100 percent DEET, brave the bugs to get a little work done, a praying mantis appears on the table in order to feast. I ask Pibi if that's the species in which the female eats the male after having sex with him. "Maybe so," he replies, "but in our country you have a bigger punishment. You have to live with her the rest of your life."

February 24—Bananal, Brazil

Hundreds of people wave from the shoreline at Belen do Solimoes. Every person on board the big boat wishes we could stop there for a little fiesta time, rather than suffer another night of mosquitoes. They radio me to ask Martin if we can stop an hour early so we can anchor the *Cassiquiari* at the village port, eat before the bugs came out, and enjoy the conveniences of the village. From our vantage point, we can see ten or so people hanging off the second floor rail of the *Cassiquiari* carrying on, tropical drinks in hand. It looks like a tourist boat.

"I will stop in the middle of the jungle," an offended Martin declares. "There's too many people on the boat. In one week, be five less. They think this is vacation. Eating. Drinking. Who pays for all these people? Tell the big boat to go away at least one kilometer. I am working. I am swimming. I don't want to see them anymore. They want to stop and have a party. They don't care about swimming. They aren't here for Martin. They are here for vacation." If there's one thing Martin hates, it's watching others have a good time while he's out busting his ass.

Our guide, Miguel Rocha de Silva, informs us we have to stop at a small station on the left bank to report to customs and clear our passports. Martin's still wound up. "Control. This is South America, not North America. This is jungle. Why you need passport in the jungle?" Martin continues swimming past the customs office, and we never hear another thing about it.

We stop for the night across the river from the small village of Bananal, having covered fifty-seven miles on the day. Martin continues his frustration at dinner. He's annoyed at the disinterested attitude of the team when nobody can find a corkscrew to offer him his nightly glass of red wine. "Give me bottle; I'll open in five seconds," he yells while miming the action of breaking the top off across the table. When the bottle is finally presented to him, he promptly mixes the red wine in a glass with orange pop. "A little spritz," he says.

Martin goes to bed early while a full sausage-fest fiesta of Brazilian dancing breaks out among a bunch of guys on the second deck. The mood is more like a college dorm than an expedition. Martin is right; some people have to go.

February 25—Nuevo Esperanza, Brazil

Our tough looking boat driver, Armundo, suddenly jumps forward from his post at the back of the boat as Martin prepares to enter the water early in the morning. He'd been startled by two Surucucu snakes that had found shelter near the motor of the escort boat. Martin shows no fear but seems slightly irritated by the delay as Armundo orders everyone back onto the *Cassiquiari* and nimbly tosses them both over the side of the small boat with a large stick. We blow off the incident as no big deal, but find out only a few days later from Miguel that those little Surucucus that we didn't give a lot of thought to were actually young Bushmasters: silent bringers of death. Armundo is very fortunate they didn't find a way into his hammock as he slept only a few feet away.

We cross paths with the Cousteau expedition, but Martin is focused on a daily mileage goal and does not want to stop swimming in order to rendezvous. They're still interested in seeing the swimmer, and send a small boat out to say hello and take a few pictures.

Twenty years ago, Miguel guided Jacques Cousteau on an Amazon expedition in order to document everything from the coca industry to the goldmines to deforestation to global warming. Now, his son Jean-Michel and daughter Celine are doing a twenty-year Amazon revisited expedition to document what changes have occurred in the last two decades.

More recently, Miguel was the guide for the New Zealand sailing champion Sir Peter Blake during the Amazon portion of his 2001 environmental expedition. Sir Peter was murdered by river pirates near the mouth of the Amazon on the eve of his departure from the region. This fact has given the team a collective lump in the throat.

Shortly after waving goodbye to the Cousteau expedition, Martin connects with a thorny stick while crawling and buries a dozen or so slivers deep in his left hand. He bleeds for five minutes, stopping swimming long enough for us to wrap it with a bandage, which falls off within ten minutes of swimming.

Martin's mood cheers up a little after lunch. He even hollers over to get my attention once to show a fake mustache he's made out of some sort of hairy plant he'd swum into. His habit of picking up sticks and examining them has diminished slightly due to the presence of critters on a lot of the debris. A few days ago, Martin swam within a few meters of a large rat who'd hitched a ride on a floating log. We've also seen many huge spiders, but it's the snakes in the boat this morning that really have him cautious of swimming into debris today.

Martin ends the day a little early after covering fifty-five miles. "Another day is done. Each day 2 percent more of swim complete. No," he pauses while looking at the sky and counting on his fingers, "1.8 percent."

A new trend has developed on the boat at dinner time. By the time Martin finishes swimming, it's dark and the open air mess hall is swarming with mosquitoes. Dinner has been coming out earlier and earlier every night. Tonight, Martin changes out of his stinky wetsuit and walks upstairs to the dining room to find the carne asada gone and the potatoes cold. "Now I see how it is. This is big vacation for everybody. Plenty of beer, plenty of food. Take a lot of pictures, stand around and do nothing all day while Martin is swimming. No more."

February 26—São Paulo de Olivença, Brazil

Martin has a quiet breakfast this morning, barely touching his food. "I have stomach problems," he informs us. "Cold potato is not good for stomach. The food sat out for more than an hour and a half while people were smoking, some people were sick. Not good for me." He informs Miguel that the food is not to be set out until he's coming out of the water, and that he will always be the first to eat from now on.

I'm appalled at the lack of respect shown to the expedition chief. The problem is that there is not only one team on the boat, there are five. The swim team, telemedicine team, film crew, satellite live streaming team, and the crew of the *Cassiquiari*. Everyone has their own personal set of priorities and is trying to find the best way to profit most off the expedition. Many people on this boat are psychologically ill-equipped to deal with three months on the Amazon, and I look forward to the inevitability of watching them crack one by one.

After living in the *Cielito Lindo* for a month, we now have more people and less space. We sleep two to a room the size of a small jail cell, and it seems like we're always in each other's way. The first few days we were all overly polite to a point of annoyance, but after living in the cramped, mosquito-infested quarters for nearly a week, tempers are starting to flare.

I'm rooming with Corrado, and we get along very well, but there is only space for one of us to be in the room at a time unless we're both in our bunks. There's no space for our gear, so it stays on our beds with us as we sleep.

I'm awakened from a nap in my cabin mid-morning to chaos and yelling. "Borut, what the hell is going on out there?" I hear

John yelling as he runs down the deck of the boat. From my vantage point, all I can see is Martin on top of Paul, flailing away with roundhouses.

Apparently, Valter would not allow Paul to board the escort boat, had grabbed him, and some sort of altercation ensued. When Paul gained the upper hand and Valter fell backwards, Martin leapt into the boat like a flying fish and pounced on Paul. Chris and the boat driver were finally able to break up the fight and get Paul off the escort boat. By the end of the day, Paul's bags were packed, ready for the next boat back to Tabatinga.

Paul apparently had a knife in his pocket; he later informs the two that next time he will use it. "Don't worry Valter," Martin says, "if he comes for me first, you'll be safe, I have two hands that are more dangerous than any knife."

There's a fat Englishman who's assisting in the satellite operations. He's another of the "Oakley types" who sit around all day drinking and playing on the Internet. Since Paul is going to be escorted to the next town via small boat, Martin sends the fat man packing as well.

Adrenalized by the scuffle and looking to make up for a day of minimal progress yesterday, Martin swims thirty-three miles before lunch. Valter is doing a good job finding current on his morning shifts; Martin tells me he's training him. At lunch, Martin shows me some damage to his hand. He claims it's from hitting a submerged tree while swimming, I think it may have been from the brawl.

At lunch, no one dares touch their food until the swimmer has his plate and is seated at the head of the table. The alpha male has made his presence known. Martin swims through a heavy rain most of the afternoon, finishing the day covering fifty-seven miles. "If I swim eighty kilometers each day," he says to himself aloud as he tilts his head and counts on his fingers, "Manaus in seventeen days. If ninety . . . okay . . . eighty-five is good."

February 27—Santo Antonio de Iça, Brazil

After a rough first day, our escort boat driver, Armundo, has been doing a great job. He's by far the most talented driver we've had thus far on the trip; able to stay a good distance from the swimmer and keep the motor running. Dark, muscular, and covered in tattoos, he smokes a few packs a day and never says a word, John has given him the nickname, "badass." We communicate almost exclusively by hand signals, sitting in the boat for hours at a time without either of us uttering a word, but we seem to get along just fine. Each night he sleeps in a hammock in the escort boat, wakes up and does a quick check for snakes, then it's all day on the river again. I don't think he even owns a shirt.

Martin is getting into the daily rhythm of the swim now. He entertains himself with long stories. Sometimes when he's on his back we'll see his lips moving and his head nodding yes and no occasionally as he makes hand gestures as if he's talking to another.

Anchoring for lunch along some thick vegetation proves to be a big mistake today. The team returns from the mess hall to find the ground floor of the *Cassiquari* teeming with swarms of red ants. All of the rooms along the bottom left floor of the boat, including Martin's has to be emptied and fumigated, but there are still stragglers making their way around the boat and some of our equipment bags are infested. Most of us have little welts all over our ankles from the tiny little ferocious biters, which are more aggressive than their North American cousins and inject a more troublesome poison.

Yoram Yaeli, a slick Israeli businessman who captains the Internet satellite team, has been going ahead to bigger towns occasionally to set up welcoming committees. He talks to the mayor, gets all the important guys from town to come out, then takes the two prettiest young girls he can find and puts them in skimpy little Indian princess outfits and has them stand up on the front of Martin's escort boat to attract attention. He's quite a wheeler-dealer and has talked endlessly about all the corruption in Brazil's political system and how he's learned to capitalize on such corruption by setting up huge promotions and making sure the right people are paid off.

I'm still having health problems. The Cipro worked for a few days, but my diarrhea is back. Maybe I'm going crazy, but I can feel something crawling around in my stomach. I've been losing weight, and now am the lightest I've been since high school. My weight this morning on the doctor's official digital scale was 142. I'm 6 feet tall and was pushing 170 when I went down the Mississippi with Martin a few years ago. It's been a month now, and I keep thinking of this fat, hairy guy I saw on Discovery Channel who had a worm in his stomach for many years. He tried everything and couldn't get the thing to leave, until finally he set a raw, bloody steak on his stomach and laid on his back in a hotel bed until the thing finally burrowed out through his skin and into the raw meat. Adding to my troubles, I've picked up some sort of infection under my tongue, around my saliva glands.

I've been eating a lot, but can't seem to keep any weight on. Actually, I'm hungry all the time. Often I find myself sitting in the escort boat dreaming of pizza, hamburgers, ice cream, chocolate, and some good whiskey.

Martin swims another fifty-four miles today, finishing amongst a mob of fans at Santo Antonio de Içá as darkness settles in. Dozens of small peké peké boats zigzag around the harbor, waiting for the swimmer to appear, and hundreds of people cheer from the sloppy bank. Martin slurps his way barefoot through knee-deep mud to greet the cheering throng on shore. He's cut off from his boat team amidst the darkness and confusion as a crazed mass leads him up a giant hill and into the town square in a scene that resembles the running of the bulls.

As navigator, one of my jobs is to carry Martin's land shoes. I'm cut off from him in the crowd and he has to walk all over town without them. When we arrive back at the boat, many of the fans jump on to try to get a closer look at him. The team is forced to leave the harbor before a riot breaks out and we disembark to find a quieter place on the edge of town to anchor for the evening. The people in this town are calling Martin "O Homem Peixe" ("The Fish Man").

February 28—Timbotabua, Brazil

Miguel has won the hearts of all of us with his gentle and kind words of wisdom. He refers to himself as a young man of sixty-six years who reluctantly left the jungle at the age of eight to receive an education. His mother, Almerinda, insisted he go out and learn about the world, then come back and teach what he learned to his family and the other people of the village. The story reminds me a bit of Plato's Allegory of the Cave, in which a young man finds a circle of light leading to the outside world, and attempts to explain to the other cave dwellers what he'd found.

Miguel has taken his mother's words to heart. He's created a foundation, Fundaçao Almerinda Malquias, whose primary function is to teach the youth of the jungle to live in harmony with their environment as their ancestors once did. Located in Novo Airão, near Manaus, the group plants an endangered tree for each new child born in the area.

The doctor has begun riding along with us in the escort boat in the afternoons. She talks to Martin in Slovene, and is always snapping me out of pleasant daydreams, asking me logistical questions. Sometimes she sits in the front of the boat and suns herself and he'll squirt water on her occasionally using a one handed motion as if he's squeezing a small ball. Today she was quizzing him on the state capitals of the United States.

The hardest part about having the doctor on the boat is that I never know what to do when I have to take a piss. She sits in the front of the boat, and if I take a leak out the back, I'll be on live web cam. Oh well, I guess they don't call it live streaming for nothing.

Having a third person in the boat slightly taints the comfortable silence that Armundo and I have developed during our long afternoons on the boat together. The sum total of our communication might be me throwing him a bottle of water or pointing left or right, and he returning with a nod of the head to show understanding. There's really no need to say anything more. The guy is the most talented boat driver I've ever worked with, and needs very little direction. As my Portuguese improves, we discover in a rare conversation we're both engaged to be married in the same weekend in July. Martin has great respect for Armundo's talents also. In fact, Armundo is the only boat driver I've never seen Martin frustrated with. Boat drivers make awesome scapegoats.

Every time we pass a little village, boatloads of people come out to greet Martin, and many line up on shore and wave. I'm not exactly sure how they know he's coming, as Internet access is pretty much non-existent. Word must travel fast along the river.

Late in the afternoon, Martin notices another troop of howler monkeys. He has a knack for hearing them before I do, which is uncanny considering he's in the water. He claims to have heard a jaguar the other day. His face contorts into a snarl of teeth as he turns his hands into claws and mimics the fierce sounds of the giant cat. I don't believe him, but he's not one to exaggerate about such things.

Martin suffers through another fifty-two miles today, ending the day a little early due to some open wounds on the backs of his legs. The constant rubbing of his wetsuit on skin has eaten away at the flesh behind his knees. There is really no effective remedy for this problem; it will get progressively worse as the swim continues, eventually spreading to every crease on his body.

Martin is still being followed by pink dolphins, and some sort of freshwater stingray or jellyfish-looking creature surfaces near the swimmer late in the day. Corrado makes the mistake of asking the tired swimmer as he exits the water, "Martin, how do you feel today?"

"I've been swimming twelve hours a day every day for the last month. How do you think I feel?" We've all learned to give Martin a little space after he comes out of the water, as he's always exhausted and not in a very sociable mood.

I spend part of the evening making some repairs to the "stupid board," which I'd sat on and cracked out in the boat, and hope Martin doesn't notice the damage. We have hundreds of thousands of dollars worth of high-tech equipment on the boat, but ask Martin and he'd probably tell you it's the most essential piece. It's only a three-dollar kids' toy, but it serves as his speedometer and odometer.

March 1—Ilha Xibeco, Brazil

After feeling sick for nearly a month, I have more strength and energy today. Today is Thursday, always my best day because the effects of my Tuesday night malaria dose have finally worn off. Getting through Wednesday is like making it past the greens and blues on a Monopoly board full of red hotels. I'm still hoping to take my first solid crap in over a month one of these days, and I hope it comes soon because I really can't afford to lose any more weight. I've been hanging on to the last of my Cipro to use as a last resort, but I'm about there now if things don't change for the better real soon.

A sheet of white appears on the horizon as the river disappears for its regularly-scheduled afternoon whiteout. Every day since leaving Tabatinga more than a week ago, we've had a fast-moving rain front move through at some time between two and six. After a mostly sunny day, a quick downpour and gusty wind come seemingly out of nowhere, then it's sunny again. The rainstorms are usually a welcome distraction to Martin and all of us on the escort boat as they help to break up the monotony and allow Martin to remove his uncomfortable mask and get a much-needed reprieve from the sun.

The sores on the backs of Martin's legs are a nuisance, but the swimmer sums it up today as he tells us, "If it was easy, someone would have already done it." Martin toughs it out for another fifty-nine miles today, his highest total since entering Brazil a week ago.

After fighting his way through half of the world's most dangerous river, Martin is sunburned, tired, and sore, but overall is in much better shape than expected. Actually, he's two days ahead of schedule. Aided by the highest water levels to flow through Peru in many years, it's taken Martin only twenty-nine days to swim

1,646 miles. The hard part, however, is yet to come as he still expects another forty-one days or so to cover a similar distance to the river's mouth at Belém, Brazil. The closer Martin gets to the Atlantic Ocean, the more difficult the swim will become as he deals with wind and waves on the bigger water, slower current, and eventually ocean tides.

March 2—Ilha do Capote

In addition to the raw areas on the backs of his knees, Martin has also developed some bone spurs where his flippers come into contact with his feet. We made some alterations last night, and he seems to be more comfortable swimming this morning.

Yoram is still going ahead at every town to contact the mayor and grab two girls to attract the locals, and his plan seems to be working. Martin Strel mania continues to sweep across Brazil as the swimmer works his way deeper into the heart of Amazonas. Martin has already reached superhero status in Brazil, and people are starting to chant his nickname, "O Homem Peixe!" or in broken English, "Feeesh Mawn!" The fish is a sacred part of people's lives here along the banks of the Amazon. It makes up the bulk of their diet, and their sustenance depends on it.

Every small village sends out a convoy of dugout canoes packed to the gills with awestruck villagers. The rest of the townspeople stand on shore on their tippytoes, frantically trying to catch a glimpse of O Homem Peixe before he quickly swims off into the horizon. Some of them run down the bank as far as they can get, and many of the children and a few adults jump in the river and try to keep up with the swimmer. None have made it more than thirty seconds or so before falling back, but everybody wants a chance to swim with the Fish Man.

They called him the Fish Man back in Peru also ("El Hombre Pez"). The two languages are just so darn similar, but to a man, none of us can understand hardly a word of Portuguese. If I talk slow enough, they can understand my Spanish, but seem annoyed at me for struggling with the local lingo. On paper the words look nearly identical, but they use all these nasal and shushing sounds that I just can't seem to grasp.

Martin swims a few miles out of his way to cross over the Rio Jutai and stop for a quick but raucous welcome at Foz Do Jutai, where dozens of children dive into the water and join him, thrashing around for a few seconds before tiring and having to return to the bank. After a quick speech, Martin jumps back into the water and continues downriver. He rides the confluence line where the clear black water of the Rio Jutai meets the muddy brown water of the Amazon for over twelve miles before the two different rivers are fully mixed. Martin swims until sundown, chalking another tough fifty-six miles off his list. We anchor for the night in the middle of a side chute, nearly a half-mile from the nearest shoreline. We hope this will keep the mosquitoes at bay, but they still come out in full force, confining us to our tiny rooms.

At dinner Martin is all business. "Today is 4.5 percent of the remaining total. Tomorrow will be 5 percent. Every day will be more. Today is finished. Tomorrow is a different day."

John convinces Chris that he will meet more girls if he gets a mohawk. Borut performs the duty in my bathroom using an electric shaver connected to a Chinese converter with jumper cables running to a marine battery. One look in the mirror and his confidence with the ladies is crushed. We think it looks great, but he's embarrassed to be seen without a hat and plans to shave his head completely the next day. What hurts him most is his theory that Brazilian girls worshipped his blonde hair, and now he has none left.

March 3—Fante Boa, Brazil

John has started the routine of joining me in the escort boat to take advantage of the last few hours before sunset and get some good video footage of Martin swimming. We're about the same age and have become pretty good friends over the course of the trip. He thinks up imaginative dialogue ideas, and I narrate for sections of his documentary while Martin swims in the background. Unlike with Paul, Martin is becoming more and more receptive to John's presence in the support boat.

His shoulders exhausted from a long day of swimming, Martin is backstroking and telling himself stories. His hands are waving, his lips are moving, and he's completely oblivious to our presence. During these moments I usually just watch Martin out of the corner of my eye, giving him some privacy to complete his inner dialogues. John decides to gamble, interrupting the swimmer to ask him what he's thinking about. I cringe.

"Ahh, stories. Many stories. Today I spend three hours with my wife, but she doesn't know it. My mother is working ten hours a day on the ranch. My daughter is finishing school. I go to visit all these people while I'm swimming. I need a lot of time to see them all. I go to visit my family every day.

"Sometimes if I have more time, I think about people on the boat. What are they doing. Are they eating? Are they drinking? Where do they live? I think of Matt's house on the Mississippi. I will go to visit him there after swimming Amazon, because many people on the Mississippi know me. I will go to see the son of his sister who was born the same week as I started swimming Mississippi River five years ago. He's a symbol for my Mississippi swim. I catch him in my hands after swimming when he was a little baby. Now he's a little man and I am swimming the Amazon.

"So I tell myself stories of my life, of my family, of the people I know. There is peace here in the jungle. Living in the city is not good for peace. All those people in L.A. need to come to the jungle and find some peace. I like to listen to the animals. Sometimes I see them, especially in the mornings. I love to tell myself stories and be in the peace of the jungle. I like it better in the water than in the boat."

I think I see tears in John's eyes. This is the Martin we wanted to know and understand. He's such a hard man to penetrate. He has such a tough exterior, and it's impossible to get close to him. But this is something from inside his soul. This is Martin Strel. I've been with Martin for hundreds of hours without getting this close, but John has a knack for tapping into a person's core.

After dinner, Martin retires to his room as John, Corrado, Chris, and I play our Saturday night Texas Hold 'Em game. Martin declines our invitation to join us. "After Belém, I will gamble with you. Now, I must rest." Actually, Martin spends most of his free time alone in his room, but he doesn't sleep more than four hours each night. He's too exhausted to socialize and too tired to sleep. Basically, he just sits there staring at the wall each night counting down the days and trying to ignore the pain.

March 4—Palheta, Brazil

Martin is probably as close to 100 percent as I've seen him since day one. His sunburn is healed thanks to the recent rains and the mask, and he hasn't acquired the shoulder problems that have plagued him in other long swims. He may be a few years older and slightly past his prime, but he knows how to pace himself for the rigors of marathon swimming. This means taking it easy every few days and swimming on his back for an hour or so to give his shoulders a rest occasionally, even though it means a slower pace. His mental health seems pretty good; the doctor takes credit with her nightly psychotherapy sessions.

Others on the boat have been getting a little edgy of late. Ever since Martin reestablished himself as the alpha male on the boat, a hierarchy of sorts has developed, and people are still jockeying for position. It's readily prevalent at the dinner table. Martin sits at the head of the table. His navigators, Valter and myself, sit to his left. I offer Valter the chair directly to Martin's left, but he insists I take it, calling me the head navigator and himself navigator number two.

Ever since the fight with Paul, Valter's demeanor has changed. He's gone from a peaceful, middle-aged man sitting with one leg crossed over the other while whistling love ballads and scanning the horizon for a good photo opportunity to a sled dog that's just heard the call of the wild. The whole idea of being on a hardcore expedition has transformed him into a tough guy with a mysterious, almost cowboy-like look in his eye. When Chris mistakenly sits in Valter's spot at the dinner table before Valter arrives, I warn him he'd better leave that spot open. Nobody else would dare sit in Valter's spot.

The doctor, who always seems to have his ear, sits to Martin's right, followed by Borut. Then it's John and Yoram, followed by Corrado and Chris. Yoram just can't wait for Valter or me to finish eating, so he can move up the line and get a chance to tout off to Martin about the receptions he's planned and whatnot. He's a sly guy, and we all know he's profiting more than anyone on this trip with all his connections to mayors and sponsors and all.

I share one of Borut's laptops with Corrado and Valter. I write the book and the website news, Corrado translates to German, and Valter sends home tons of pictures every night. We've been pretty civil with one another with the sharing, but Borut lets them know that the book has priority, and sometimes I have to requisition the computer from one of them and they get a little bitter toward me.

In addition, Yoram and the other satellite guys have started disconnecting us from the Internet, especially the doctor. They say that our big uploads are taking away too much bandwidth from their capabilities to offer live streaming. They're sometimes sneaky about this and claim that the Internet isn't working, when it's just disconnected. Yoram comes to me the first day he pulls this and says he can secretly offer me a "twenty-minute window" of Internet access each day, but I have to keep it a secret, especially from the doctor, whose telemedicine uploads are slowing down the whole system.

John and his crew have at times gotten under people's skins with their constant videotaping and manipulation of the boat. Personally, I think it's fun to look forward to seeing us all on a movie and participate in any way possible, but others don't appreciate his creative genius, especially the doctor.

John has also had disputes with Yoram over contractual issues surrounding the cameras and the right to tape Martin, and he's looking for a chance to remove the banners from all Yoram's sponsors, as they "kill the jungle mood for the movie."

Everyone has their own personal agenda on the boat and sometimes we butt heads a bit. I've taken to writing the expedition news in my own room, as everyone has something they want me to add. The doctor always wants me to say something about telemedicine, and Yoram wants me to go into detail about each town, the mayor, and his sponsors. I've taken a territorial approach to writing the news, sticking to the exciting parts of each day and not worrying about keeping everyone else happy.

Martin is swimming late in the afternoon when he notices a foul smell. The rotting carcass of a huge crocodile is floating nearby, with three vultures hitchhiking a ride. We judge it at about fifteen feet long, although it's been dead for a while and the head and tail have both been chopped off, possibly by poachers. We don't stick around long, as the rancid odor makes us all feel ill.

Martin has his best day of swimming since entering Brazil. After a strong morning, he declares to us all at lunch, "I will swim 100 kilometers today." Sporadic afternoon showers keep him sheltered from the sun, enabling him to do more freestyle swimming. He keeps up the fast pace until a few minutes after sunset, finishing the day at 101 kilometers (62 miles). The current is slower here than it is in Peru, and we were afraid those days of over sixty miles were behind us, but Martin proves us wrong.

March 5—Baronesa, Brazil

The river is as big as we've seen, as we're often miles away from the nearest shoreline, then we realize it wasn't even a shoreline, just another island, and the shoreline is another three miles behind the island. I have a big responsibility as navigator, as I choose our routes through the islands based on what I predict will be the best current and most efficient path. Sometimes the big boat disagrees with my decision, but ultimately, I have the final say if I'm in the escort boat with Martin. It really doesn't matter if they disagree, but if Martin suddenly wonders where the current went, I have to answer to the man.

We aim for a point of land about six miles in the distance. It seems impossible to reach, but in an hour or so we're there, and picking out another point of land on the horizon to aim at. Every once in a while we get lucky enough for the main flow of current to come near land. These are the rare moments I look forward to all day, and the expectation of such moments usually causes me to change my navigation strategies to bring us closer to shore.

Martin enjoys these peaceful moments too. We kill the motor, I paddle, and we talk a little and listen to the jungle while Armundo sits around chain-smoking and looking tough. The cries of howler monkey troops are almost always present; they sound like a wind that has suddenly kicked up, but with a deeper, scarier tone. The birds make screeching and whistling sounds way out of proportion to their little bodies. The sounds of the jungle are soothing. There's no development for hundreds of miles in any direction. We're so alone here. Sometimes we hear mysterious growls and whoops. Martin tells us that in the early mornings before sunrise, the noise is ten times as strong.

It's rained every afternoon for the last eleven days. Every time I see a storm front on the horizon, I ask Martin to predict how long it will be until it rains. Then I make my prediction, we bet a beer on it, and I set my stopwatch to see who wins. I owe him a lot of beers. I think he could be a meteorologist when he retires from marathon swimming. He wouldn't need any computers or radar, he could just swim in a lake and tell you what the weather would be for the next few days based on the sky and how the air feels.

Martin suddenly stops and motions for us to be silent. We all hear a low-pitched growling noise: "EEEEEEEEEEEEE-ROWWWWAAAAHHHH."

"Jaguar." Our Brazilian guide warned us putting one finger to his lips in a hushing motion. "EEEEEEEEEEEEEEEEEEEEEE-EEEEEEROOOWWWWAAAAHHHHHH." It calls out again from the nearby foliage, this time a little louder, and a little angrier. We all go completely silent. The foliage rustles, we hear some sort of crackling noise like a deer in the woods, but see nothing.

The jaguar is an endangered species, but thrives in the Amazon region. It's a solitary hunter, preying on fish, frogs, and small alligators near the riverbank. Closer to villages the jaguar will occasionally sneak into town at night to feast on dogs or livestock. Deforestation, ranchers protecting their stock, and poaching of the valuable hides have caused the future of this stealthy predator to be in jeopardy.

After pushing forward another fifty-seven miles, Martin entertains us all at the dinner table with his low, throaty, growling, jaguar imitation. He can also imitate a howler monkey quite well.

Dr. Latifi is back. That means now I'll have two doctors pressuring me to mention telemedicine on the expedition news every night. It doesn't take him long. "Hey Matt, we love the news, everyone thinks it's great, but don't you think you could mention more how Martin's swimming will help to bring the wonders of modern medicine to the primitive world?" He had bought a bottle of Johnny Walker Black and makes the mistake of leaving it in the kitchen while John, Corrado, Chris and I play poker. That's like leaving a piece of raw meat on the street near a pack of hungry dogs and walking away. Sorry Dr. Latifi, the bottle didn't survive the night.

March 6—Tefe, Brazil

Great, malaria pill day again. Some of the team has been slacking on their doses. We all take different kinds of pills with different side effects. Mine include nausea, vomiting, strange dreams, visual hallucinations, and hair loss. In addition to the malaria pills, we've all been immunized for yellow fever, typhoid, hepatitis A, hepatitis B, tetanus, and meningitis. All of us complain about the side effects of our pills. All of us except Martin.

Sometimes I have to remind myself that this fifty-two year-old man in the water next to me has been swimming for thirty-four days, and will be swimming for another thirty-six days. He just continues swimming, and we all take what he's going through for granted. Today he broke the 2,000 mile mark, making it the third-longest swim in world history (the first, second, and fourth-longest are all his, too), and he still has more than a month to go. This isn't a man in his prime, but a fifty-two-year-old with a big belly who loves wine, beer and bratwurst. I look down at him and see him suffering mile after mile after mile, and I can't believe he's actually swimming the Amazon. Nobody thought it was possible, and he's doing it. This middle-aged guy with a body like one of the Belushi brothers is swimming the Amazon.

How lucky am I? I'm here in a boat, witnessing one of the greatest athletic achievements in the history of the world. I'm going down the Amazon, realizing one of my last unfulfilled dreams. It's so easy to get caught up in the daily grind and forget about how lucky you are to be at the place in life you're at. But then I just kill the annoying motor and paddle a bit, listen to the symphony of the jungle, and find myself living entirely in the moment.

Today the goal is to reach the village of Tefe. We plugged it into the GPS three days ago, and the entire boat has been abuzz about it since. Before that it was Fonte Boa, Foz do Jutai, San Antonio do Iça, and Tabatinga. Tomorrow it will be Coari, Anori, Manaus, and finally, Belem. All just dots on a map and strange names I've never heard of, but these alien names have captured our entire focus as we count down the miles to each name, pass it, erase it from our minds forever, and aim for the next town on the map.

When one person gets sick on a boat, the whole boat gets sick. The latest is a strong case of the common cold. First a few of the Brazilians, then Corrado, then John caught it, now I have it. We know how Martin feels about illness, so whoever isn't feeling well stays away from him. Corrado takes over my afternoon shift today while I nap, cough, and sniffle. Corrado is over his bout, but I can hear John suffering in the next room. The doctors tell us he has early stages of pneumonia, and will be resting for the next week. Corrado informs me that Martin swam another sixty miles today. The team stops for supplies and medicine in Tefe, and is currently anchored outside the small village of Porto de São Francisco.

March 7—Sáo Francisco

I spend another day in the infirmary, confined to my room reading, coughing, and sneezing. I finally find time to read the copy of *Heart of Darkness* I brought along. The other book I brought was *Huckleberry Finn*.

As I sit in the room, I hear a lot of coughing and wheezing going on around me in the boat. I theorize that having a doctor on board takes away from the mental toughness of the men on the team. Unlike other expeditions, we have a safety net of sorts under us, and know that if we do get sick, there is help available. If there was no help available, we wouldn't get sick. Hospitals are full of doctors, and everyone there is always sick. The doctor isn't happy when I share my theories with her.

Martin is currently healthy, while everyone else seems to be sick. Regardless of how hard we try to avoid him, it's a small boat, and inevitably he'll get sick too. No matter how sick Martin gets, he'd continue swimming. He has to. To quit for him would be to die. He has the whole country of Slovenia depending on him, and now half of the world is watching. He'll suffer through everything, but he'll never quit.

Sometimes I watch him swimming when he's in especially rough shape, and I think about Prometheus who angered Zeus when he gave man fire. Zeus chained him to a rock and let an eagle slowly peck out his liver. Martin is like Prometheus, being chained to this river and counting down the kilometers to when he can finally end his suffering. He looks at each day as a percentage of the total kilometers remaining. Since he started that train of thought we've moved from 1.8 percent to about 6 percent as each day's total represents a larger fraction of the constantly shrinking remaining kilometers. Martin has always had a thing for numbers.

Corrado does my shift again today. He says he enjoys being back out on the river with his old friend Martin from their time together on the Yangtze, and it gives him a chance to take some good pictures. He doesn't bother taking my raingear as it's a beautiful day.

The glassy water mirrors the sky as Martin reenters the river after lunch on a cloudless, windless afternoon. Two hours later, a wall of black clouds appears on the horizon, the wind kicks up out of the East, and a sheet of rain swallows up the swimmer. The team radios the escort boat to return to the boat for safety, but Martin refuses. It's too early to quit for the day, and he'd set a goal to make Coari by tomorrow. The visibility becomes so bad that at one point Martin gets disoriented and begins swimming upstream.

Afternoon storms have been the norm since Martin has entered Brazil, but today is the most severe we've seen. Storms come out of nowhere on the Amazon. Luckily, this one blows over quickly, and Martin is able to cover fifty-four miles on the day.

March 8—Coari, Brazil

It's hard to believe we've been on the river now for thirty-six days. Time is all messed up in my head. Peru and the *Cielito Lindo* feel like years ago. The fourteen days we've spent in Brazil aboard the *Cassiquiari* feel like a lifetime.

Feeling a tad better after two and a half days of rest, I rejoin Martin on the escort boat, cautious not to let him see any coughing, sneezing, or sniffling. My bowel movements have become solid again for the first time since January, a fact I'd love to jump on the top deck of the boat and happily scream out to the world, but I'll just have to tell all of you.

Maybe it was being away from Martin for a day, the halfway point of the trip, or feeling a little better, but for the first time on the expedition, the significance of Martin's swimming is beginning to crystallize.

The Amazon River is the jugular vein that supplies the lifeblood of the world. It's the lungs from which the world breathes. Here, we're like microorganisms swimming through a human body, trying to find its heart; trying to reach the heart of the planet.

Illness continues to spread on the boat. A portion of the team has been quarantined to the confinement of their own room as a wave of illness plagues the group ranging in severity from the common cold to symptoms of bronchitis. The concern is to keep those infected away from the swimmer so as to ensure his health. The doctor has been busy going from room to room to treat the sick and offer medicine and moral support. Martin is still healthy as an ox, and swims fifty-seven miles today, ending near sunset at the bustling port of Coari.

Currently, we're anchored near a floating barge of cattle. It takes three men to push them off into the river one at a time to where they're dragged by canoe to the butcher on the next floating raft. The whole process is barbaric and might make me think twice before ordering my next burger at a fast food restaurant. A thorough investigation of the meat-market-on-barrels called Coari finally yields me the two things I've craved most for the last month: whiskey and chocolate.

March 9—28 de Julio, Brazil

It's a very quiet morning onboard the *Cassiquiari*. Martin and Valter are out in the escort boat with one of the Brazilian guides,
while barely a soul stirs on the big boat. Half are ill and confined
to their rooms, while many of the others are a tad hung-over or
at least a little tired after a night of fiesta at Coari.

Thankfully, everyone who left the port to enter the town was
smart enough to carry a light and survived crossing an old wooden
bridge that had huge, gaping holes where the wood had rotted
away every few yards. The best strategy was to keep one's headlamp on the path ahead while precariously tiptoeing across the
main support beams.

"The air is different today," Martin tells Valter early in the
morning. "It won't rain today." Martin turns out to be right as the
day proves to be the first rainless day on the river for the swimmer since entering Brazil two weeks ago. Martin comes in after a
long morning of swimming to find the usually crowded lunch
table nearly empty, and sends Valter out knocking on doors.

While some of us are nearly over our illnesses, many of the
others are attempting to hide the early symptoms. I notice Pibi
and Chris both holding back the sniffles and stepping away from
the table after quickly eating to release the coughs and sneezes
they'd been retaining through the meal. To a man, when the doctor asks one of us listed among the healthy how we're feeling, the
answer comes back, "I'm great. Fine. 100 percent." John had to
stop at a hospital a few days ago for chest x-rays and antibiotics
and the doctor has been able to keep his symptoms from progressing into a full-blown illness. After three full days alone in his
room with Chris bringing him meals, he occasionally makes an

appearance on the deck of the boat. Miguel and some of the Brazilian guides are now among the ill.

I come out for my afternoon shift to find that Armundo is not at his post in the boat. He's also sick. Great, now I have to train another rookie in the art of guiding a marathon swimmer. Paulo is very timid at first, following the swimmer rather than leading him. After a few hours of hand gestures and broken Portuguese expressions, he gets the hang of it, although he still isn't nearly as confident as Armundo, and we don't have nearly the rapport.

The river today is usually approximately four miles wide, with only a band of about 100 yards of swift current. The object is to find that 100 yards, and stay in it. Martin trucks along at six to seven miles per hour as long as he's in the flow, but suddenly I'll look down and we're doing three or four, and the current is nowhere to be found. A careful investigation of the speed of floating debris to the right and left usually aids us in rejoining the fast water. You have to be constantly on your toes to keep in the fastest current at all times in order to make the most miles possible each day. After a slow start to the afternoon, Paulo catches on quickly, and Martin makes fifty-eight miles on the day. The current seems to have picked up a bit in the last few days, maybe due to all the rain we've been receiving.

I watch Martin swimming on his back near the end of the day in a rare moment without his mask. He closes his eyes and grimaces as if praying or immensely concentrating on something of great importance, then suddenly snaps out of it, opens his eyes, looks around to see where he is, then just as quickly returns to the grimacing concentration. He looks to be in a great deal of pain, but due to his stoic nature, he won't complain. The more it hurts, the quieter he usually gets. I caught a glimpse at the back of his legs as he took off his wetsuit. They're completely raw from rubbing, and every other crease on his body is beginning to show wear. He's lost thirty pounds.

March 10—Anori, Brazil

Miguel radios us with a strange urgency in his voice. He informs us that there is an emergency and we need to return to the *Cassiquiari* immediately.

The Anori Police had boarded the *Cassiquiari* at approximately 4:00 PM after receiving an SOS call from a large boat that had been attacked by a band of river pirates. The *Cassiquiari* was drifting near Martin and the escort boat, and had no idea what the police were talking about; they were even hesitant to allow the police onboard until their identities were confirmed. A similar boat in the immediate vicinity had sent out the SOS after coming under assault in broad daylight. The police were still unable to locate the pirates or the raided boat. Martin and I recalled seeing the other boat drifting along the opposite bank a few kilometers earlier, but didn't see anyone aboard.

River pirates on the Amazon are professionals. They have faster boats, better guns, and more modern equipment than the police, and sometimes pose as the police in order to surprise their victims. Vast distances between towns or any legal influences have created an atmosphere on the Amazon for banditos that is similar to the Wild West days of raiding trains and stagecoaches. There is nothing out here to prevent the crimes from occurring.

We anchor for the night at the port of Anori. I don't understand the psychology involved, but none of the team seems the least bit afraid of the pirate attack. Personally, I'm petrified. The pirates could just have easily have raided us as the other boat, and it was nothing but dumb luck that saved us. There is a tone of adventure among the men on the boat tonight after the news. "Oh, pirates. Wow." It's as if pirates are a thing of a Hollywood movie with patches and parrots and peg-legs. It just doesn't seem to sink in to the team that today's pirates carry automatic weapons, not swashbuckling swords. Pibi is running around with a patch over his eye and a machete trying to scare us all. Maybe we've been on this boat for too long.

Since arriving on the *Cassiquiari*, I've taken Miguel's lead at all times. The man was born in the jungle and has been guiding on the Amazon his whole life. If he's nervous, I'm nervous. He was the one who first told Martin and me the news of the raid, and I could see by the sincerity and urgency of his eyes that it was no joke. He'd already lost a close personal friend to river pirates on this river, Sir Peter Blake, gunned down during a 2001 environmental expedition; he didn't want to lose any more. Thankfully, he had retired to his bed by the time Pibi started his buccaneer dance.

After a few beers, someone points out the lights of Anori on the horizon, and has the bright idea that we go find a discotheque. After some more whiskey and a few more beers, the idea sounds great to everyone. Borut, Chris, Valter, Corrado, Pibi, Aldo and I hop into Martin's little escort boat, and set off toward the lights of Anori. We have to go up a small, flooded river approximately three miles to reach the town. We bring our headlamps and plenty of beers.

The motor dies, then we flood it. Borut paddles with a broken paddle until Aldo finally gets the motor going again. Pibi starts yelling something about a fish in the boat. We don't believe him, then another one jumps in. In total we have to excavate seven slippery silver, ten-inch fishes from the crowded little boat.

The bright red eyes of crocodiles reflect off our beams, which aren't bright enough to navigate properly. We have just enough light to see the glowing eyes and part of the silhouette before the crocs slither back into the water. The river has turned into a big swamp, and although we can still see the city lights, every canal seems to turn into a dead end with a big crocodile guard. Distracted looking for eyes, we suddenly come upon land. At that moment we discover the boat had no reverse. The guys in the front of the boat take the brunt of the punishment as we crash into the edge of the jungle, but not a beer is spilled. All seven of us have to teeter-totter from side to side to keep water from pouring into the boat. And then I remember the pirates. Whose bright idea was this, and how in the heck are we going to find our way home?

March 11—Nazare, Brazil

The team barely makes it back to the *Cassiquiari* before Martin saunters up to the mess hall for breakfast. If anything, last night served as a great team-building experience, as a new camaraderie seems to be developing among the group. For once we all did something together and stayed together all evening. I say we (the team) without thinking to include Martin in the list, but one has to realize that Martin is either swimming, eating, or sleeping. He does not have the luxury of a social life on expeditions. By the end of the day he's exhausted, and after sitting at the dinner table with his team for an hour or so, he retires to his room to try to block out the pain. Sometimes we almost forget about him because his routine is so defined; he behaves at times like a machine: breakfast at 5:30, swimming by 6:00, lunch at 12:00, stop swimming at 6:00, dinner at 6:30, rest, and repeat. He's counting down the days, the kilometers, and the minutes now.

Valter, after a night of nearly no sleep, does his usually stellar job of guiding Martin to nearly thirty-seven miles in the morning. Valter has turned into Martin's right-hand man now and is always at his side, on the river, or at the dining table. He tells us at lunch that the current was over six all morning. It was our best morning since Peru.

As Martin swims on his back during the peak hours of afternoon sun, he busts out laughing several times as he tells himself stories. I pretend not to notice so as not to disturb his self-dialogue, and the sporadic laughter continues for nearly an hour. Martin is happy. I can't tell you what he's thinking about, but I'd have to say that the increased currents we found today have put him in a great mood. The current has been slowly declining since we left Atalaya thirty-nine days ago. This is the first increase we've seen, and gives Martin some hope for a strong ending to the swim.

Martin struggles through the wind and waves of a late afternoon storm to distance himself another fifty-eight miles from the site of yesterday's pirate attack. Looking for the safest place possible to anchor for the evening, we choose a religious commune of seventeen families of vegetable farmers just downstream of the small village of Nazare.

At first the commune seems to be an abandoned ghost town. We toss out the anchor rope at an empty old church made of old boards with holes cut out for windows. It seems there is no one in sight, but soon a few little brown heads pop out from between a rectangular gap between boards to peak at us. We hear a few giggles. The church is offering safe vibrations. Borut and I have been looking for a chance to walk in the jungle for the last month, but ever since those guns were pulled on us back in Peru, I've been afraid to leave the boat. The boat is a safe haven. Who knows what the jungle has in store for us?

A few of us set out for a sunset jungle hike. A well-worn trail from the church seems like an obvious route, so we start off into the jungle. Corrado, Borut, Chris, Pibi, Valter, and I come across the first hut after only a five minute walk. An older gentleman with a straw hat sits outside reading a bible while five little shirtless children run into the house and peek out the windows at us, giggling occasionally.

Each five minutes brings us to a similar dwelling, with acres of vegetables planted in sporadically cleared sections of jungle along the way. At first I feel as if we are invaders to this little utopia of happy, curious people, but everyone we come across smiles warmly and encourages us to explore. We cross paths with two extremely pretty young girls around the age of eighteen along the trail. Chris tries to engage them in conversation, but their fear and modesty gets the best of them, and they quicken their pace toward the church.

Darkness sets in and we return to the boat, but after dinner, a ceremony of sorts starts at the old church. A man near the entrance beckons us in, and we sheepishly enter. The scene is something out of the book of Acts. Men take turns giving Martin Luther King Jr.–type speeches while older members of the audience lift their hands skyward and chant in what sounds to be some sort of tongue. A silence ensues for an endless moment, after which some of the older ladies take up a chant and every single person in attendance raises their hands to us with open shaking palms and joins in the chant as they direct all of their spiritual energy toward us. Tears well up into my eyes and I almost fall over.

After the ceremony, we get some signatures with photos as required documentation for the Guinness World Record verification. Chris insists that we take the two girls we'd seen along the trail back with us to the boat, along with one of their brothers and a strapping young man of about thirty years old. After a few Cokes and some Portuguese translation, Chris develops an amazing chemistry with the prettier of the two girls. About the same time, Borut makes the mistake of offering the strapping young man a beer. I'm not sure if he'd ever had a beer, but he drinks it fast, and asks for another one. Chris is still vibing with the pretty young girl. He's grabbed a laptop and is eagerly showing them American movies.

A whole new world is opening up for these sheltered people. I sense trouble. After two hours, I look outside and see that nearly the entire congregation of the church service has gathered under a grove of trees and is talking in raised voices, gesturing toward the boat. The youngest of the priests has a desperate deer-in-the-headlights look and seems to be the center of the discussion.

It's definitely time for the girls to leave, but they're enthralled with Chris and his laptop. They tell us they want to leave with us on the boat. After pulling Chris off to the side and knocking him over the head a few times, we finally convince the two love birds to part ways. They promise each other to meet again in a year.

The vegetable farmers are relieved to see their daughters exit the boat. God only knows what they imagined might have been happening onboard. The strapping man, however, refuses to go. He insists that he will work for free if we allow him to stay with us. Miguel needs a few more hands and obliges. Later he tells us that the pretty girl was the daughter of the high priest and was betrothed to be married to a young acolyte who was considered by many to be the future leader of the church. The strapping man was offered up to us as a concession to work for free in order to let the girls go. The only problem for the future leader of the church is he doesn't have Chris's deep blue sparkling eyes, blond hair, Californian cool confidence, or laptop; Chris is dead-set on returning in exactly one year to start a new life.

The upper Amazon.

Final weigh-in
before the start of
the swim in Peru
on February 1, 2007.

Martin gets a thick layer of lanolin applied to his body before the first day of swim in Atalaya, Peru.

Martin gearing up for the first day in Atalaya.

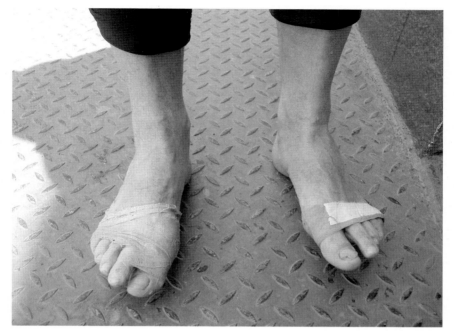

Dealing with foot abrasions.

Martin enjoying red wine and pasta at the end of the day in Peru.

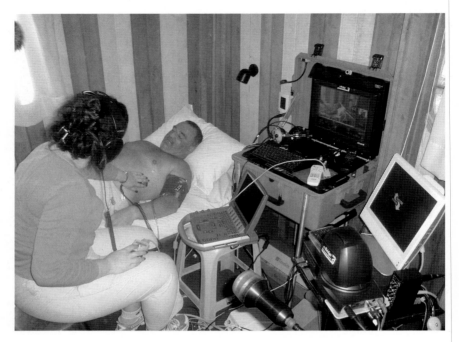

Team physician Dr. Mateja de Leonni Stanonik monitors Martin in the *Cielito Lindo*.

Martin arrives in Tabatinga, Brazil, on February 23, 2007 to much media fanfare.

Martin swimming with fascinated Brazilian escorts before the city of Jutai, Brazil.

Fans touching "human fish" hero in Santo Antonio de Ica in Brazil.

Martin consuming Planet of Health's Spring of Life energy drink through his sun protection mask.

Martin fighting with the wavy Amazon three days before the end.

From left to right: river navigator and author Matthew, boat driver Armundo, and one of the security guards with the machine gun.

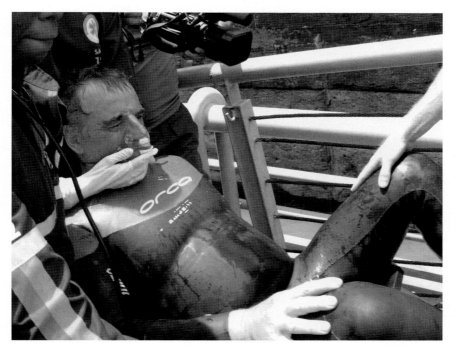

Martin, exhausted, receives oxygen immediately after his finish in Belem, Brazil, on April 8, 2007.

Martin as a twenty-nine-year-old snake lover.

March 12—Manacaporu, Brazil

Chris informs us at breakfast that he's in love, is done chasing girls for the duration of the trip, and will return to the commune in exactly one year. The strapping man from the commune busies himself around the boat, frantically cleaning and tidying everything in sight, trying to make himself look as helpful as possible.

We had anticipated a short day as we were only thirty-five miles from Manacaporu and have a big reception planned for the afternoon. We are also meeting a journalist and photographer from *Maxim* magazine, and another camera operator is joining us to replace Paul.

Martin has been having some problems with cramping in his legs after lunch. He typically scarfs down his meal in fifteen minutes, lays down for twenty minutes, and then returns to the water. Today, he eats dinner, then quickly returns to swimming before his muscles can tighten up.

Thinking he's found an opportunity to rest his aching muscles after stopping a few hours early, Martin is dragged onto the stage to join a hoard of Brazilian dancers at a large reception in his honor in Manacaporu. While Martin is on the stage, the *Cassiquiari* drifts down the river without a working motor. We've heard rumors among the Brazilians that she's in rough shape, but we're not sure exactly what the problem is. She's taking on excessive amounts of water, and we don't know if she'll hold up much longer.

With a little free time near dusk, some of the team goes on an excursion up into some dark backwater swamps off the main river and we see many large crocodiles. We miss out on a lot of the wildlife because we're too far out in the main channel, so such opportunities for exploration are a real treat.

After dinner, the new camera operator, James Clauer, is found in his room shivering with feverous chills. He'd complained of some stomach problems earlier and went in to take a nap. After examining him, the doctor takes him straight to the hospital where they find he's acquired some stomach amoebas and will have to stay for two weeks. John and Chris go to stay with him for a few hours and tell us the conditions were extremely scary, with malaria and dengue fever patients everywhere. John is upset because now that James is in the system, he'll probably get stuck there and get left behind from the team. He lasted less than half a day.

March 13—Ilha Maria Antonia, Brazil

Corrado and I are awakened at 5:00 in the morning by the nasal mutterings of loud, drunken Portuguese directly outside our room. He opens our door to find the culprits and discover it's our favorite boat driver, Armundo, and the new strapping guy from the religious commune. They're both trashed and carrying on, pressuring us to join them without any inkling of the impact their noise is having on the sleeping occupants of the boat.

A sleepy Miguel appears momentarily, and when he sees the drunken state of his crewmembers, he's noticeably displeased. I catch bits and pieces of his conversation with them; he fires them both on the spot. I'm not concerned about the strapping guy leaving, in fact I figured he'd have to go, but I don't want to lose our boat driver. Armundo has been an asset to Martin with his intelligence and decisiveness in the escort boat, and I don't want to deal with training a new guy. After pleading my case to Miguel, he obliges to allow Armundo to stay on the boat. Armundo, however, being rebellious by nature, will have none of it; he just cracks open another beer and plops down on the deck of the boat in a reclining position and stares at Miguel with a slightly defiant indifference.

Corrado and Chris come out to see what is up, and the three of us work on Armundo to get him to accept Miguel's second chance. Armundo is still adamant on leaving, and Miguel tells him to sleep on it and decide when he sober up. The strapping man offers much prayer and supplication toward Miguel, but when he's found with an open beer in the cleaning closet during breakfast, he's left on the shore.

Many of us on the team enjoy a little buzz after a hard day on the water, but none of us has been intoxicated to the level of Armundo and the strapping man. We like to tip back a few, but there is a line that we all know does not get crossed, because every moment is a potentially critical moment, and one drunken move can sink the whole ship. I know I tend to drink a little more back home in Wisconsin whenever I get caught in a rut, but not here. It's much different than the American concept of sitting around all night ingesting small amounts of poison in an attempt to free yourself from a miserable existence. Here, we have nothing to escape from; we're enveloped in the ultimate reality every moment of every day. I think it will be hard for all of us who last the entire three months down here to readjust to everyday life again.

It's a dead calm day with torturous heat. At one point I think I see rain on the horizon and ask Martin how long he thinks it will be before the rain hits. "No rain today, only high humidity. Tonight, big rain, but no rain today."

"Twenty minutes maximum," I tell him as I throw on my rain gear. I offer to bet him a beer and he laughs at me. After my twenty-minute window comes and goes, I realize the rain I thought I'd seen is just a hazy byproduct of the heat and humidity and I owe Martin another beer; I've only won one of our bets thus far, and I owe him about a twelve pack now.

Martin is now three days ahead of schedule. He has to stop swimming early again today after covering only forty miles. A big reception is planned for Manaus tomorrow afternoon, and he has to slow down so he doesn't get to the city a day early. Martin is still having problems with skin abrasions from rubbing on the wetsuit, but he is in better shape than expected after forty-one days of swimming.

We have some writers and photographers from the States onboard the boat, and Martin has been strutting around after swimming in his towel with his chest out and a beer in one hand, making all the new boat passengers aware that he's the alpha male in the group. They ask him the same questions he's heard for years, and he gives the same performance. "Hah, you think it's easy to swim Amazon, join me for one day. Who pays for all these people to eat? Who pays for all this equipment? I must be swimmer, businessman, doctor, lawyer, all at the same time."

The team anchors in a beautiful lagoon along a gradient where a clear black river slowly mixes with the muddy Amazon. One of the guides shows us his ability to call out to crocodiles and amazes us at the annoyed responses he receives from back up into the nearby swamps. Many of us are hooking up our laptops to work after dinner, when a swarm of bugs unlike anything we've seen moves in on us, completely covering our screens and clothing.

We find that as long as all the lights are off, the slight breeze keeps them away, but the moment someone turns a computer or light on, they're everywhere. With no computers the team is lost. Back in Peru, I was thankful to get one chance every ten days to send out a quick email to my fiancée and parents to say hello and let them know we were still alive. Now that we have big Internet satellites on the roof of the boat, I find myself "needing" to check my email at least three times per day. Many of the team are at the verge of panic, not knowing how they'll spend the evening without their blessed laptops.

Ultimately, the bugs teach us a great lesson. Turn off the damn computer, grab a beer or glass of whiskey, and regress into the world's oldest pasttime: storytelling. A group of us sit on the roof of the boat until the wee hours of morning, enjoying the stars, the breeze, the mysterious noises from the jungle, and one another's company until a lightning storm finally ends our fun.

Sometimes I wish we didn't have any computers on the boat at all. It seems like that would make the trip more pure. We have Martin's swim being broadcast live over the Internet at all times, but the system is getting crashed by storms nearly every day. The weather here is highly volatile, often wreaking havoc on our technology. I guess that when nature battles computers, nature always prevails. We have a full staff of computer geeks onboard, and they always figure it out eventually and get the system back up and running . . . at least until the next storm hits.

March 14—Manaus, Brazil

Martin swims through the largest confluence of two rivers in the world today, in terms of flow volume. The clear black waters of the Rio Negro join the muddy waters of the Amazon at Manaus and the two rivers run side by side for nearly 120 miles before mixing completely. As he approaches the confluence, Martin's escort boat is bombarded by other media boats, and we have to get a little aggressive in order to protect the swimmer from all of the other vessels crisscrossing in front of him trying to get the perfect shot of the swimmer.

Adding to the pandemonium are seven Brazilian champions who decide to race Martin for the last three miles of the day. They're all competitive swimmers who'd proven themselves victorious in everything from the Pan American Games to Iron Man Triathlons. Hardly fair considering they're fresh and Martin is just finishing his twenty-fourth mile of the day. The swimmers are all strong, but swimming in an Olympic pool is much different from swimming in the Amazon River. After a mile some have to be picked up by other boats while only a few are able to stay with the Slovene. Martin is the first to touch a huge media barge brimming with journalists from all over the world waiting to receive the swimmer.

We receive a major culture shock at Manaus. After two months in the jungle, we walk through a perfectly manicured garden area with sculptures and artwork to enter the five-star Tropical Hotel. I instantly feel as if I'm suffocating, and long to be back in the jungle. Sure, it's beautiful, but all of the jewelry stores and white people speaking English make me feel as if I'm back in America again, and it depresses me.

A few of us walk around and find a little pizza joint on the waterfront. We listen to a man play soft classical Brazilian music as we scarf down the first pizza we've had in about nine weeks and enjoy the scenery of massive amounts of sexy, scantily-clad females milling around the area. Several attractive young ladies beckon us over to join them, making some rather unsubtle gestures. We're a little bummed when we realize that the entire waterfront is actually crawling with high-class prostitutes preying on the rich businessman of the area like a pack of vampires. It's definitely time to return to the jungle.

March 15—Ilha La Grande Eva, Brazil

The media hordes we'd encountered yesterday have all printed their wares, and the team sits around together pointing out one another and laughing at each other's pictures on the front pages of several Brazilian publications. Martin especially gets a kick out of one that claims he must have some sort of divine connection with a medium or some sort of wizard who calms the raging river out ahead of him and keeps all the nasty predators at bay.

Martin leaves town at 9:00, while a buzz circulates through the team that the *Cassiquiari* is indeed in trouble and will not be able to handle the rough waters of the wide, windswept river awaiting us. Some even suggest that she will not leave Manaus.

The hours pass, and while the mechanic works in the space below the boat, much of the team kills time with a game of cards. We also have to wait until the boat receives clearance to leave the city. After being in the first real city after two months in the jungle and with Martin already way out ahead of us, we are all itching to get back on the river.

While the boat is being refueled and getting a few last-second repairs, government officials delay the boat's departure from town due to paperwork clearance issues. By 10:00 PM, the *Cassiquiari* is finally fixed and heading downstream from Manaus at full speed, not having had any radio contact with Martin for the last eight hours. Martin had left town in the morning, expecting the rest of the team to catch up to him by early afternoon for lunch. It seems like a repeat of the Pucallpa troubles with the *Cielito Lindo* is inevitable.

At 11:00, we receive a broken radio contact from Valter, but all we can pickup is a fractionated GPS coordinate and something about a hammock and a small village on the map that really isn't a village. We're not sure where Martin had found shelter for the night and what he'd found for food, we just hope that some villagers in the remote area through which he was swimming were kind to him, and offered some sort of assistance. We project him to be approximately fifty-two miles downstream from the city, and by midnight we're still heading slowly downstream, scanning the shoreline with a spotlight and desperately trying to make radio contact with him, hoping the batteries on their radio haven't gone dead from trying unsuccessfully to find us all day.

March 16—Itacoatiara, Brazil

A little after midnight, everyone on board the *Cassiquiari* is thrown sideways as the boat comes to a sudden halt after impacting the bottom. She's grounded, and we're still eleven miles away from the unofficial GPS location we pieced together from the last broken radio contact. The two small camera boats push from one side with their motors floored, trying to free the beached *Cassiquiari*, all the while constantly scanning in a huge circle and jamming a large stick into the mud, looking desperately for deeper water. She'd move a few meters, and we'd all get our hopes up, only to get stuck again.

After an hour and a half of this slow progress, we're free. The captain had chosen the wrong route around an island in the confusing darkness, but after a little skill from the Brazilian guides in the small boats and a little luck in finding deeper water, we're back on the main channel and approaching Martin's projected location.

After frantically searching the pitch black shoreline with a spotlight for the next hour and unsuccessfully trying to radio Martin, we finally find the swimmer at 3:00 in the morning. He and Valter are tucked away on shore, attempting to stave off the mosquitoes while sleeping in shifts on the small escort boat as the other watches for signs of the larger support boat. Luckily, the broken GPS coordinates we'd received at the last radio contact were nearly accurate, and the two savvy expeditionaries were able to recognize the hum of the *Cassiquiari's* engines and set off a flare to reveal their location.

Valter tells us that a family from a nearby hut had come down to investigate their presence, had offered them some fruit and bread, and even invited them to their home. They'd warned Martin that it was to dangerous to sleep in the boat and insisted they join them for the evening in the safety of their home, but Martin didn't want to chance having the motor stolen by pirates in the night, and wanted to keep watching for the *Cassiquiari*. They also told him a story of one of the members of their family who'd fallen off a canoe many years ago. They said he went under the water and never came back, even though he was an expert swimmer. They believed he was taken by some sort of monster from under the water, and none of them would swim in the area since the occurrence.

Although most of us expected Martin to be extremely angry for the logistical breakdown, not much is said about the incident by the swimmer. He goes straight to his room and wakes a few hours later at the normal starting time while most members of the team sleep in well past breakfast after a nearly sleepless night.

The morning is highlighted by Martin swimming past another large confluence. After winding through the jungle for approximately 1,860 miles, the Madeira River joins the Amazon about ninety-three miles downstream from the confluence of the Rio Negro. Although the swift Madeira River is longer, actually one of the twenty longest rivers in the world, the Rio Negro is much larger in width and has one of the largest volumes of flow in the world. In total, the Amazon has over 1,100 tributaries, and as with any large river system, many regions claim their river to be the true source of the Amazon, which is another reason the river is called so many different names in so many different places. For instance, although you could say we've been on the Amazon for the last forty-four days, you could also say we've traveled the Rio Tambo to the Rio Ucayali to the Puinahua Canal to the Rio Maranon to the Rio Solimoes to the Rio Amazonas at the confluence of the Rio Negro at Manaus.

Martin capitalizes on strong currents to swim another 112 miles in the two days since leaving Manaus, ending the day with a warm reception at Itacoatira. After dinner, the team gets James back from the hospital after his bout with stomach amoebas, but has to put another one in an ambulance. Dr. Leonni Stanonik went into anaphylactic shock after an allergic reaction. By the time the team gets her to the hospital she's in the beginning stages of respiratory arrest and delirious. She's out of eminent danger now, but will have to remain in the surgical intensive care unit overnight for monitoring.

March 17—Urucurituba, Brazil

The team is relieved to have the doctor back with us after her frightening experience from the night before. Most of the group had gone out to see the nightlife in Itacoatira, and were unaware she was gone until returning to the boat late in the evening. Martin himself had to carry her to the escort boat, up a steep flight of stairs at the port, and into a taxi in order to reach the emergency room in time. He'd also waited at the hospital until the doctors assured him that she would be all right. We're told that if he hadn't acted so quickly she'd have been in serious trouble, and if the incident had occurred in the jungle, she'd surely be dead. She rejoins the team at approximately 6:00 this morning, goes into her room, and rests all day.

Martin starts a little early today, and swims a few minutes later than normal; he had a goal in mind. He began the day 82 kilometers shy of 4,000 on the expedition, and 85 kilometers short of his Guinness World Record total of 4,003 kilometers on the Yangtze River in 2004.

The currents are a tad slower than normal, but Martin struggles on, ending the day at sunset just a few kilometers upstream from Urucurituba after swimming ninety-two kilometers. Everyone aboard the support boat is fired up about the record, but Martin looks very tired. After a month and a half on the river, his body is starting to show the toll the river has been forcing him to pay. His eyes are red and swollen with huge bags under them from being in the dirty water all day. He's lost so much weight that he has excess flaps of skin around his upper torso that hang strangely down, giving him a very unswimmerlike appearance. When Martin gets excited about some strong currents or the sight of a pretty woman, his face lights up and he looks like a little kid; today he looks like a tired old man. Martin's facial appearance is always changing based on his level of physical depletion. Sometimes the young man emerges from the old man, at other times, the old man emerges from the young.

The team toasts the exhausted swimmer at dinner for his accomplishment, and he appeases our enthusiasm and marks the moment by playing us all some of his favorite country-western songs on his Peruvian guitar. When someone asks him to sing along, he just laughs.

Paulo brings in some cacao he'd found growing on shore. This orange, mini-football–shaped, squash-looking vegetable is sliced open to reveal sweet, slimy-white seeds covering a bitter, purple nut. After much processing, it becomes mass produced as chocolate.

The guitar playing, wine drinking, and cacao eating ends early as Martin warns us not to start celebrating too much yet. "I still have almost a month of swimming, and from here to Belém things will become more difficult and much more dangerous." With that, he finishes his glass of wine, recases the guitar, and retires downstairs to his sleeping quarters.

Tonight some of us decide to check out the town of Urucurituba. The small little village is centered around a beautiful, white stone church, and the whole town is laid on a chunk of granite. People of all ages sit on benches in the square outside the church laughing pleasantly with one another and playing a game of bingo.

I sit on the roof of the boat under a brilliant panoramic of stars, sipping on Johnny Walker Black as a distant lightning storm slowly eats the southern sky. Raven-sized vampire bats swoop along the rippling surface of the Amazon, gobbling up insects. For a moment I worry about my throat and imagine one swooping in to attack me, but the irrational idea passes quickly and I again lose myself within the turquoise vibrations on the surface of the water. I think of all the kind people in the little village of Urucurituba. I close my eyes for a moment and think of God. I think about the contrast between the beauty of the river and the ugliness of the diseased prostitutes and drugs of the cities. The souls of all twenty-two people onboard the *Cassiquiari* have converged here and now in this land that could be heaven or hell; and Martin just keeps on swimming.

As I'm completely enveloped in the peaceful moment under the stars on the roof of the *Cassiquiari*, a commotion on the shore breaks me out of my tranquility. A man in an orange shirt is being physically beaten by a rabid gang of about ten other young men. He breaks free from the pack and runs like a frightened rabbit up the side of the river while the pack of wolves pursues.

March 18—Boa Vista, Brazil

The team is greeted by a new member today as Igor Ogorevc from Planet of Health joins us on the *Cassiquiari*. I was under the impression that he was Martin's personal trainer, but that vision quickly fades as I watch him sit across from Martin while hypnotically swinging a blue topaz pendulum and fiercely concentrating on the motion for a full minute without blinking. After a short pause Igor declares Martin to be in excellent health besides a slightly low sodium level, and calls him one of strongest human specimens he'd ever examined.

Igor uses the pendulum to project energy from his mind as he scans Martin and other team members' brains and physical bodies. "The mind is the strongest energy in the universe," he tells us. "Anything is possible with the mind." After arriving at a diagnosis, he uses natural oils, extracts, and specially prepared waters to bypass the symptoms and directly treat the source of whatever ailments he's divined.

The entire team is flabbergasted and confused about this strange diagnostic system. Over the course of the day we're all examined by Igor and his blue topaz pendulum. I am told I have a high acidity level in my stomach, and am given a corrective potion. He also tells me my pancreas is working too hard, probably due to my meeting with Johnny Walker on the roof last night, and rubs a few drops of oil #19 on my chest as a remedy. After fifteen seconds I feel my stomach releasing energy from my center, up into my head and out of my hands. The whole experience makes me feel slightly stoned. As I watch him perform readings on some of the other members of the crew, I can't help but think back to stories I'd heard of the great prophet/healer, Edgar Cayce, who turned the medical world upside down one hundred years ago.

Igor explains that everything he does is based on temperature, pressure, flow, and time. "It's all physics," he assures me. "Modern medicine has had its chance, but I am the future." Similar to homeopathic medicine or even a shaman from the jungle, he uses natural oils and extracts to treat unbalances in the body. What I really don't understand is the swinging of the pendulum.

"I'm scanning your brain using my brain. I am the computer, the pendulum is only the printer." I'm still not sure what exactly Igor is. He acts like a seer or a medium, and his methods are something a water diviner would do, yet he dresses like a businessman, wearing a short neat haircut and a polo shirt. I'm still a little perplexed, but Martin tells me that if I have any problems at all, Igor can fix me within ten minutes.

Martin's equipment is starting to take a beating. He blows out a flipper today and luckily has a spare on the boat. Now he wears one blue flipper and one yellow flipper. His wetsuit is completely hashed, but he says it's comfortable and after trying a new one for the day, he plans to finish the trip in the shredded one. The crease where his upper legs meet his groin area is utterly raw and causing him a great deal of pain. He applies an ointment after swimming and grimaces from the resulting burn.

Martin's lips are still split from being constantly chapped from the sun. It's the one place that the mask doesn't cover. He explains to me today that because the river runs from west to east, the sun is always directly in line with the river. On the Mississippi, a north to south river, the sun moved across the sky crossways. This theory gets me thinking, but I guess I can't disagree with it.

With every grueling mile extending his new world record by one, Martin entrenches himself another fifty miles into the history books. We have a hairy moment while passing some red rock cliffs as the swimmer is caught in giant whirlpool and spins around helplessly for thirty seconds. Even the escort boat loses control for a moment, and turns around in circles. By the time we reach Martin and throw him the rescue chord his adrenaline had kicked into overdrive and he'd used his powerful arms and legs to thrust himself out of the whirling tornado threatening to suck him under the water. Nearly any other swimmer would have lost his life.

Meanwhile, the team onboard the support boat was experiencing a completely different crisis. A frantically tearful father raced toward the *Cassiquiari* at full speed in a small boat, screaming in Portuguese and pleading for help for his dying daughter. The thirteen year old girl had fallen from high up in a tree and had been impaled with a sharp limb from near the ground. The large stick had entered her midsection via the vagina, causing serious internal wounds. Dr. de Leonni Stanonik performs an emergency surgery, saving the girl's life.

March 19—Parintins, Brazil

We've had a running joke on the boat about Pibi that he looks more and more like Tom Hanks from *Castaway* every day. He's the only one on the trip who hasn't shaved his beard, and it's getting thicker and grayer every day. At lunch today someone makes a new comparison, calling him Ernest Hemingway. The new nickname causes quite a row with the team, and looks like it might stick.

We'd acquired new river navigation maps at Manaus, and as I fold one up after lunch, Martin cautions me. "No Matthew, not like that, like this," he demonstrates. "These maps are impossible to find. You can't get these maps. Very expensive, you must know someone in the Brazilian military to get these maps. I will save these maps and bring them home with me, be very careful." While still reprimanding me about the maps, he starts in about my chewing tobacco. "Matthew, that stuff is very dangerous for you."

"And swimming the Amazon is very dangerous for you," I retort.

It's a calm afternoon and Martin is zigzagging through some heavy debris when he points out a huge log, one of the large, proportionate types they use for logrolling competitions up in Hayward, Wisconsin. Being from Wisconsin, I've always been intrigued with the sport, and feel compelled to give it a try. I ask Martin if he minds, but he doesn't understand what I'm talking about as I run in place on the deck of the boat to demonstrate while making a spinning motion with my hands. He catches on and beckons me into the water.

Logrolling is next to impossible, at least for me. I can barely stand up on the log, much less run on top of it. After about five attempts, all of which end with me falling precariously into the Amazon, sometimes bouncing off the log in the process, I give it up and cling to the log trying to catch my breath. Martin laughs hysterically at the process, and soon he tries to get up on to the log with me. He just barely gets on when the resulting shift of weight throws us both into the water again. He pops back out of the water immediately to remount the log, laughing the whole time and inviting me to join him again on the log.

We soon realize if we both mount the log from opposite ends, we can counterbalance like a teeter-totter. After a few minutes of getting used to the log, we're both able to stay on much easier. The kid in Martin is really coming out, and suddenly he places one elbow on the top of the log and challenges me to an arm-wrestling match. I slither up to his position and we lock palms, but before he can overpower me into the water, we both spill off the log once again. More laughter ensues. Martin's playing.

"Again, again," he exclaims. I'm a pretty good arm-wrestler for a little guy, and I'm able to hold my own for nearly half a minute before Martin puts my wrist down again, and again, and later with the left hand.

"Now, Hulk Hogan and Jesse Ventura wrestle," he challenges as he straddles the floating log. "Last man on the log wins." I hop back on the log easily now. Balancing on a log in the Amazon is comparable to snowboarding or surfing, absolutely impossible on the first try, but you start to pick it up after a few ugly attempts.

We both square off from opposite ends of the log and snail our ways toward the middle. When we get into range of one another, he immediately delivers a head slap that sends me reeling, but I stay on the log, then another, then, he somehow gets hold of the back of my head and drives me face-first into the log before I finally lose my balance and drop off. Wrestling with Martin is like wrestling with Lenny from Steinbeck's *Of Mice and*

Men. He's having a blast, sure, but the man just don't know his own strength.

OK, so this is how it is, I think as I hop back on for a rematch. This time I won't let him get so close to me where he can use his power. I'll use my quickness. My lip is already fat and bleeding from the inside, and looking down, the metal on my whistle has been bent into an unusable position.

Again we approach the middle of the log, but this time I keep my distance. Martin is about eighty pounds heavier than me, but I have a longer wingspan, so my goal is to use my reach to beat him. Two months on the Amazon River with Martin and three expeditions of serving the chief have mounted up to this one moment where I can exact a little revenge.

I bob my head like Muhammad Ali, just out of reach of his slaps, waiting for the opportunity to strike. After he misses, I lunge in with a left and catch him squarely on the side of the head, surprising him completely and sending him off the log.

"This is my log." I yell at him as I slap it with open palm behind me as if slapping a horse in the ass. "You'll have to come back and take it from me." Martin was no longer laughing, and suddenly I realized what I'd just done. *Ah crap, I'd slugged the chief and now I'm taunting him.* I'm balancing pretty good on the log now, and am sure I can use the same strategy to beat him again, but beating him might not be good for my immediate future.

The third and final battle, the rubber match, starts the same. We both mount the log from opposite ends and slide up toward the middle. There is no more laughing now though; things have gotten a tad serious. Again I keep my distance, using my right to faint a fake jab, then coming back with the left to head slap him, but he's a savvy fighter, and is ready for me, catching my left wrist just before the point of impact, pulling me in and then pummeling me with his free hand. I try to land a few shots with my right, but am basically helpless once he has me in his grasp, and I have to use my only free hand to try to cling to the log while he waylays me. I make it for a few seemingly endless seconds before he finally peels me off into the muddy water.

I am a little nervous that I'd pissed him off earlier, but I can see plainly from his beaming smile and outstretched hand on the top of the log that he's content to have won the final match and isn't the least bit angry. "Good fighter, Matthew," he tells me as he offers to shake my hand. I notice my watch is missing, now somewhere on the bottom of the Amazon.

Martin swims fifty-one miles today, finishing at Parintins, a town reputed by many Brazilians to have a carnival that will give Rio a run for her money. The first thing we see as we land on the town docks are a group of transvestites who invite us to join them on a smaller boat that is docked nearby.

After dinner, some local government officials take us on a tour of the festival grounds. The arena is full of huge, mechanical Styrofoam creatures manipulated by men hidden inside of them. It's a fantasy land of animation, and Martin walks around looking into the sky like a little kid at Disneyworld. He has even more fun when some of the controllers allow him to take over. He climbs to the top of a giant mechanical tiger and rides it around the arena, he dodges the charges of a huge toro, and boxes with a female version of the Jolly Green Giant.

After the festival grounds, seven of us get into two taxis to go to a discotheque. Seeing white people in the car, the cabbie immediately finds a station with American music. The first song was something by Madonna. The second was, "It's raining men, Halleluiah."

"You like?" he asks us proudly while bopping his head to the music, obviously with no idea of the meaning of the words. Without asking us our intentions for the evening, the taxi driver makes a cell phone call, stops outside a house where a pretty young girl comes out, they have a quick conversation, then she runs back into the house and we drive away.

After driving past many other great-looking bars, we arrive at the discotheque. The discotheque was really no different than any other bars besides the fact it had a little spinning five-dollar disco ball hanging from a string on the ceiling, and a television on a table hooked up to speakers playing Bee Gees music videos continuously. After only about twenty minutes at the discotheque, the same young girl who'd talked to the cabbie shows up at our table, dressed to the nines, with six of her friends. None of the girls is over the age of eighteen, while at thirty-two, I am one of the youngest in our group.

Prostitution here seems to have no negative connotation. It's just a side-job, and any girl who approaches us over the age of fourteen seems to be on the take. Many young women work normal jobs during the day for low pay, and in the evening, there is nothing taboo to them about earning a few extra dollars as creatures of the night. Martin had warned us all before the expedition that although the predatory fish and reptiles of the Amazon were dangerous, the most dangerous creature of all is the woman, as disease is rampant in many of these parts. I don't mean to bash Brazil, because I'm sure it's not like this everywhere in the country, but when twenty-two men land at the port of a small town, word travels fast that there is new money to be had, and we're almost always swarmed by prostitutes.

Most are just sweet, innocent looking young girls of sixteen or so who aren't full fledged whores, they're just capitalists who'll spend eight hours with a guy and ask him for twenty dollars at the end of the night. They're sweet, they're cute, they look harmless, yet they're dangerous as hell. The best strategy is to shoo them away quickly before they can get any false notions of profit. Plus if you spend too much time talking to them, the desperation of their situations makes one truly sad.

March 20—Juruti, Brazil

After spending the last twenty-five days swimming through the Brazilian state of Amazonas, Martin enters the state of Para. The illness that plagued the team a few weeks ago has finally run its course and we're a fairly healthy bunch again. Martin wants to make it to Santarem on Saturday to attend a big reception, and plans to start a little earlier each morning to reach his goal.

Martin pours himself a glass of Mead as we wait for lunch to be brought out. When he looks down into the glass and back at the bottle, he sees that the fermented honey drink is loaded with ants. He grunts, shakes his head, and drinks it anyway in one continuous swallow. The stuff was very expensive, and he didn't want to see it wasted.

As usual, lunch is brought to the table in five large platters, each containing a different course. "Five things here," he tells us. "In America, they give you a hamburger and say thank you very much. There's no such thing as American food. American food is Italian, Chinese, and Mexican. Mexican food is good, but Slovene food is four times better."

The wind starts whipping up from the east after lunch and Martin is continuously pummeled by giant waves in his face. There is a lot of debris in the water here, and some of it's really hard for me to see with all the big waves. This is dangerous for Martin, and stressful for me. All it takes is one mistake to ruin everything.

Our small escort boat is taking a thrashing and I'm getting queasy as the boat rises and crashes, but we'll have to face conditions like this every day now as the water continues to get bigger and bigger as Martin closes in on Belem. Looking back, I see the *Cassiquiari* is getting tossed pretty hard in these giant waves today also, and I'm a bit concerned about her as well. There are still rumors of her filling with water slowly and constantly needing to be pumped out. As another giant wave crashes into the side of our little boat, I notice we only have one life jacket onboard. I've only seen a few others on the *Cassiquiari*.

Looking for a point of land to help block the wind, I can no longer see the shoreline in front of us or on our left, only endless horizon. It's like we're on the ocean. Finally the town of Juruti appears in the direction we're headed. After an hour it looks close, but is still nearly twelve miles away. Martin finally reaches the town near sunset after covering fifty-three miles on the day.

March 21—Obidos, Brazil

With all of the heat and bugs, some of us have been having a hard time sleeping lately, and when Igor overheard a few of us talking about it at dinner last night, he showed us a pressure point near the left nipple that he says controls sleeping functions. I went into my room for the night, placed my thumb on the pressure point, and was zonked out in five minutes, sleeping soundly until morning.

It's one of those perfect, dead calm days on the water, a little hot, but the type I love nonetheless. I think the sky here is more beautiful than in North America, maybe due to all the moisture in the air. It's a softer blue with shades of indigo, yellow, pink, and purple with little dreamy clouds that float by so close it looks like you could touch them.

At another horizonless spot on the river, approximately six miles wide, Martin starts reminiscing about some of the lakes along the Mississippi River.

"Ah, Matthew, big lake here. Makes Pepin look small, even makes Winniebigoshish look tiny. Lake Bemidji was a nice lake, small but very beautiful." He goes on to name off several of the towns he swam through along the upper Mississippi, counting on his fingers as he names them off. "Bemidji, Grand Rapids, Brainerd, St. Cloud, Minneapolis, Red Wing, Winona, La Crosse, nice towns, but Mississippi not so big now, huh?"

As we approach Obidos, the tranquil day is threatened by a storm approaching from upstream. Martin points out some red rock cliffs near the town and tells me, "There near those cliffs is the deepest place on the whole Amazon. 100 meters." The storm is closing in on us fast, and the *Cassiquiari* radios to us that they're going to shore to anchor and seek shelter. I can see sheets of rain and dark clouds on the horizon and am a bit concerned about our safety, but Martin waves one hand away and says confidently, "Don't worry Matthew, the storm will miss us." I disagree, bet him a beer, and spend the next two hours hoping the sheet of rain will catch up to us as it slides off to the South and we continue downstream at approximately six miles per hour. At one point I can see the *Cassiquiari* about three miles away, getting pummeled, yet we're dry, always staying just a mile out ahead of the storm front. Martin arrives at the beautiful town of Obidos after swimming fifty miles on the day. The rain finally catches us as we anchor near a lush green hillside for the night.

Igor continues to impress all of us with his knowledge and unorthodox techniques. He points out the place on the chest cavity that he says houses the soul, and tells us a story of saving the life of a man that had been left for dead by modern medicine, merely by caressing his soul for one hour. He also shows us some stress relief pressure points, and I can immediately feel the difference when he presses on the spot.

Igor tells us he also has an ability to mentally prepare water, or change it into any substance he wants. He tells us a story of a time when he and four friends went out for a friendly dinner. Four of them were drinking a beer, while the fifth had an orange pop. As a joke, he says, he transformed the pop into whisky. The man finished the pop, ordered another one, and was soon dancing and singing and carrying on to such a degree that he began to disturb the other patrons of the restaurant. Another time, he tells us, he and Martin were driving when Martin suggested they stop for a glass of wine. Not wanting to stop, Igor merely turned the bottled water Martin was drinking into a substance consistent with red wine. We all guard our water a little closer now that Igor's on the boat.

March 22—Boa Vista, Brazil

Today marks Martin's fiftieth day of swimming. Valter guides Martin another forty-five kilometers before lunch today. He's developed into probably the most valuable member of the team now, after starting the expedition as "cook's helper." The transformation of Valter on this journey has been amazing, and has not gone unnoticed by other members of the team. He's gone from peacefully humming love ballads to becoming the man with the thousand yard stare. We have a running joke where he offers me the seat to Martin's left, calling me navigator number one, but I refuse to take it, offering it back to him as navigator number one. Without Valter taking over navigational duties for the long and tiring morning shifts, I'd never be able to write this book.

Martin struggles through a fierce headwind with huge waves breaking across his face most of the afternoon. Progress is becoming slower as the river widens each day, sometimes to more than six miles across. After a rough afternoon, the wind finally dies down a bit for the last two hours before sunset. Two sailboats greet the *Cassiquiari* as she looks for a place to anchor for the night.

Ever since our log wrestling battle, Martin has developed a thing for logs. He likes to swim with them for a few meters, examine them, and compare them to things. Today near dusk, he finds one that looks like a horse, saddle and all, and swims beside it for nearly twenty minutes. At the end of the day, he gives it a heave downstream in the strong current, waves goodbye, then turns to me in all seriousness and says, "My friend is going to reach the Atlantic. Maybe we'll see it again tomorrow."

March 23—Upstream from Santarem, Brazil

Rough water limits Martin to just twenty-four miles today. The support boat is being tossed around like a toy, dangerously taking on a lot of water, while Martin is getting pummeled relentlessly by huge waves when he finally submits for the day. "Enough is enough, tomorrow is another day." The aches and pains are starting to add up after fifty-one days of swimming, and Martin decides to use the afternoon to rest his weary body. The timing is perfect as Martin is still ahead of schedule, and a large reception in Santarem tomorrow will give him another partial day of swimming and more of an opportunity to reenergize. We're hoping the day and a half of rest will allow him to recuperate a little for the last three weeks of swimming, which will be by far the most difficult.

His main physical concerns are continuous cramping in his legs and terrible chaffing problems wherever the wetsuit makes contact with the skin. The creases at his Speedo line on the top of his legs are completely raw. He applies an ointment every night after swimming, and calls out in pain when it makes burning contact with the skin.

One pleasant surprise is how well his shoulders are holding up. The strong current has allowed him to swim a few miles each day on his back, saving his shoulders for the end of the trip. By this stage of his Mississippi and Yangtze swims, his shoulders were completely shredded, and he needed a masseuse and some strong pain medication just to get back into the water each day.

I've noticed lately the more exhausted Martin gets, the more polite he is toward his team. When he's fresh and energized, he does a lot of yelling, but when he gets run down from day after day of swimming, he's more apt to talk less, and when he does, he uses odd expressions like, "thank you," "please," and "you're welcome." Tonight at dinner, I see a first. When the flan comes out, he grabs a big knife and a stack of plates and starts passing it around like a birthday cake. Maybe he just wants to cut us all extra small pieces so he'll have more left over for himself, I'm not sure.

Miguel tells us a story about a recent guiding trip in which he and some American clients went to visit an old man who lived alone in a hut in a remote part of the jungle with his pet toucan. The American nature lovers offered the man fifty dollars to let the bird go free. This being a huge sum of money for the man, he was just about to release it when Miguel stopped him and pulled the Americans aside. This man had lost his wife, he'd lost his children, and he lived all alone in the jungle, his only friend being this toucan. If they paid him to let it go, he'd let it go, but then he'd probably die of loneliness within the year. The Americans reconsidered, told the man to keep the bird, and gave him twenty dollars for his trouble.

March 24—Santarem, Brazil

Today is a day of rest for Martin as he swims only five miles before attending a ceremony in Santarem. I'm startled by fireworks as we approach the main dock where the entire town seems to be fighting for position to catch a glimpse of the burly swimmer. Martin touches the shore and immediately disappears in the mob. An orchestra begins to play as I try to follow Martin down the street but can't fight my way through the mass of people. He's finally led up to a podium in the town center.

The Mayor of Santarem, Maria Do Carmo Lima Martins, and the Vice Governor of the State of Para, Odair Correa, give a large reception to honor the swimmer, then we all go out for an extravagant dinner. It's one of those fancy restaurants where a guy comes along with a big hunk of meat and a huge knife. You stab the piece you want with a fork, and he slices it off. We're a pretty ragged looking bunch and are getting some strange glances from the upper-class clientele.

One of the frustrating but necessary parts of expedition life is pleasing the sponsors and appeasing the public relations people. Someone has to pay for all this stuff and they need to have big events like the one in Santarem to see where all their money is going.

I can't wait to get back on the river, and I can tell by looking at Martin, that although he's smiling and shaking hands, he wants the same. After fifty-two days on the Amazon, going through some of the most remote areas on the planet, city life is suffocating, and all the formalities that come with meeting dignitaries and dealing with media seem completely superficial.

I'm dirty and smelly, in need of a shave, and have been wearing the same clothes for two months. Yeah, I feel the eyes of the fancy folks in the restaurant cutting into me, wondering what right I have to corrupt their elite dining experience, but I don't care. I'm on an expedition, I'm hungry, and some rich suit is paying for it all, so I think I'll have another glass of that expensive red wine that tastes so good.

After devouring as much red meat and wine as humanly possible, I notice the buzz has gotten around the room a little that "fish man" is dining with the Vice Governor. Faces go from condescension to curiosity as they make the realization.

As we return to our anchored boat, a few straggling fans try to catch a glimpse of the swimmer as we walk down the dock. Young boys are fishing in the moonlight near the *Cassiquiari*, catching piranhas one after another on cut bait. Martin retires to his room quickly, hoping the added rest today will allow him to catch his second wind.

Miguel and the doctor become engaged in a serious discussion this evening. Apparently, we're entering into the most dangerous area of the entire Amazon. The region of Para in the remote areas downstream from Santarem is infamous for pirate attacks. Miguel tells us we'll come up an ambush point where the river narrows in a few days. They also come in silently by the cover of night in multiple canoes, throw big hooks up to catch the boat, and then storm onboard, overpowering the team.

Miguel insists we put four armed men on the boat as a precaution, but Borut is concerned about money. These men would need to be paid, fed, and need a place to sleep in an already crowded boat. I go to sleep with the issue still unresolved.

I recently traded rooms with Igor. Although the room I gave up was much more comfortable, it was in the most accessible portion of the boat, the first door behind the captain's quarters. The one I took over in the basement is in a dark, damp cubbyhole, tucked away in the most unreachable part of the boat. It leaks like crazy, smells of septic, and you needed a headlamp to find the door, but all this talk of pirates has gotten me paranoid, and I figure it will be the last place they could reach. Some of the men on the boat talk of how they'll be swinging machetes or canoe paddles or whatever they can find, but I bet if it ever came down to it, most of us would be hiding under our beds with the doors locked.

March 25—Curua, Brazil

I wake to the hum of the *Cassiquiari's* motor as we leave port. It's a relief to finally leave the modern city of Santarem and get back into the jungle. Coming upstairs, I see some new faces. Three husky dudes in red paratrooper uniforms are standing around rigidly in the mess hall. Although I sense a lot of negative buzz about the space, food, and money issues, I am secretly quite relieved.

Martin is admittedly tired today, even after his day and a half of rest. "I ate too much in Santarem," he tells me while holding his gut. "My mistake. Santarem is a good town, but too much rest and too much food. Now it's hard to swim today." I am a little shocked to hear Martin complain about being tired. Martin never complains, so I figure he must REALLY be tired.

At lunch, Miguel points out a giant Iguana in a tree. It takes three of us five minutes of scanning the tree with binoculars and digital cameras to find it, even though he spotted it easily with the naked eye. The thing is huge, maybe four feet long, but its green and black body match perfectly with the tree, and if you look away for a moment it's harder to find it. Many other team members come up to get a glimpse but become dismayed when they can't locate the reptile. Some of them don't even believe we'd seen it.

When Martin is tired like he is today, he doesn't say much in the water. He tells himself stories. I watch him swimming on his back, his lips moving all the time and sometimes he even uses hand gestures. He's not here on the Amazon today, not even close.

> *He's eight years old, at his family's small chicken farm in the village of Mokronog in old Yugoslavia. He's hoping to get his chores done early so he can ride on his new bicycle, as his mother had promised him. She's in*

the field with him. He wonders when his father will come home. He wants to go visit his friends down the road on his bicycle, but first he has to feed all these chickens.

A series of sudden, sharp blasts from my whistle steal this pleasant daydream away as Martin narrowly misses swimming into a half-submerged log. I try to use the whistle sparingly, because I realize that when Martin is swimming, he can't think about swimming. It's impossible to swim twelve hours a day and think about swimming twelve hours a day. You've got to go to another place. My whistle is a teleportation device and time machine all rolled into one. It brings him twelve thousand miles over the Atlantic and forty-five years into the future back into the present moment. . . and at times he hates me for it. He goes from basking in the joys of his youth to having his entire body burning with pain as he swims hour after hour, mile after mile, day after day, engaged in one of the most challenging feats in history.

Martin's progress is notably slower today. He grimaces more and talks less, always a bad sign. The more vocal Martin is, the better he feels, even if his vocalizations seem hostile, it's just his way of blowing off steam.

The wind and waves are relentless again today, but the tired swimmer is still able to battle through another forty miles. There aren't a lot of towns left on the map between here and Belem. We should reach Monte Allegre tomorrow. Martin and Borut have put April seventh down now as their new target date to reach the Atlantic, but there is a lot of rough water between here and there.

March 26—Monte Allegre, Brazil

Martin's pace is a little better, and the tiredness that plagued him yesterday seems to be less of an issue today. Maybe he needs to just get back in the rhythm again. It's hard for an endurance athlete to stop and then start up again, they need to keep going and going.

At lunch today, Martin surprises us by cracking a few jokes. When Igor doesn't arrive to take his chair and someone asks where he is, Martin replies, "He made himself disappear." Later, someone compares Borut on camera to Matt Damon. "Hah," Martin laughs, "Borut looks like Matt Damon. Yah. Matt Damon at five in the morning."

Martin tells us he's been cramping up a little after lunch due to overeating and intends to eat a bit lighter for the duration of the trip. "I can eat ten times more, but it's better to stop," he tells us as he walks away from the table. His weight loss has stabilized after losing thirty pounds so quickly, and he's only dropped a few pounds since.

The doctor spots a crocodile on shore and radios to warn us not to get too close to a nearby island. Miguel told us a story last night about two friends of his, brothers, who were fishing together from shore. The top to their cooler blew into the water, and one of the brothers swam in to retrieve it. A giant boil erupted on the surface, a huge crocodile thrashed, and the man disappeared. Later, the other man returned with a gun and killed the crocodile to retrieve the remains of his only brother. Miguel still has the skull of the crocodile at his home. The croc was fourteen and a half feet long.

The river is so vast now it looks like we're on the sea. Martin is swimming through a maze of islands, and it's hard to tell exactly where we are on the map or whether the shoreline to our left is actually the shore or just another island that will disappear and reveal the true shoreline to be another six miles in the distance. Anytime the support boat stops at a town for gasoline, repairs, or supplies, finding it again in the labyrinth of islands becomes an all day affair.

Martin uses a new swimming technique for the first time in three expeditions today. In the late afternoon, as the waves are starting to subside a bit, he flips back onto his stomach and starts doggy paddling, continuing this method for an hour or so. It's quite a sight: a fifty-two year old fat man wearing a white mask and a huge floppy ladies hat, doggy paddling toward the Atlantic Ocean, somewhere beyond the limitless horizon.

Despite some mid-day waves, conditions are far better today than yesterday, and Martin swims forty-five more miles, ending the day just downstream from Monte Allegre.

A man pulls up in a dugout canoe to sell us fish after watching the team anchor in the slack-water near his family hut. Appalled to see a man swimming in the region, he warns us the area is loaded with flesh-eating piranhas, and relays the following story to us:

> *A two-year-old girl was sitting quietly near the shore while her mother did the family's laundry in the river a few feet away. Looking up from her scrubbing board after hearing a commotion, the mother had her worst dreams come true. By the time she got into the knee-deep dark water and grabbed her child by the wrist, it was already too late.*

He's the father of the girl who was killed. He pleads with Martin to only swim in the swiftest part of the river. Later, to test his story, I throw out a chunk of meat on a fishing line. My twenty-five pound test Spiderwire is instantly shredded. A feeding frenzy ensues every time the meat hits the water. The things are rabid for my bait, but impossible to catch. I throw on a steel leader after breaking off a few times, but then the issue becomes setting the hook into their impenetrable, ironclad jaws. After hoisting a few half out of the water only to have the hook pop loose while my fishing skills are scrutinized by the rest of the team, I finally get one up over the rail. Later, Martin comes along to see the action. I hand him the pole and he curses like a Slovenian sailor as he unsuccessfully tries to hook one of the little carnivores.

Tonight is our weekly poker game. I want to invite Igor to play, but John and Chris don't think it will be fair. I think as long as we don't allow him to use the pendulum it will be okay. We need the new blood. Corrado, a poker regular, recently finished his section of the expedition, and we lost Paul and Jamie nearly a month ago. Still, they vote against it.

Our poker nights have become more than just cards, it's turned into a little American Powwow session of whisky drinking and tobacco chewing in which we all feel like we're back in the States again. Also, it's a good time to get the latest gossip on the boat. Hushed conversations have been floating around amongst different members of the team. . . subtle tensions that I'm not privy to, but through the rumor mill, usually our late night weekly card playing sessions, everything comes out in the wash.

The latest are rumors of Miguel leaving the boat due to personality conflicts and money issues with the Strels, the doctor threatening to leave due to Igor's presence, and contractual issues between John and the Strels over such trivial issues as paying for the gas on the camera boats. The two groups, John's and the Strels', have a symbiotic relationship, but there's been talk of not allowing cameramen on the escort boat until John forks over more money.

March 27—Praihna, Brazil

Borut has been under a lot of stress lately. Contractual issues and sponsorship concerns have really got him worried, and it shows on his face. He looks like he's aged a few years since the trip began. It's late in the swim, and he doesn't want to bother Martin with all of the red tape, political BS of the expedition. Martin is just about swimming now and Borut doesn't want to break his concentration, so he tries to solve all the problems single-handedly.

As expedition leader, he has to handle all of the tough logistical problems of the trip, and people are always pulling him away from his work to ask if they can get online for "just five minutes," or make a quick phone call on his satellite phone. He's also the one everyone goes to when they have a problem with their computer. It's kind of sick when you think of it: middle of the darn Amazon, and we all have a computers, satellite phones, and web cams. It just doesn't seem right. I enjoy reading stories of Shackleton and other old school expeditions, and to think of all this technology on the boat makes me feel a little impure.

It's another windy morning, but the wind lets up after lunch for a few hours, only to pick up again later in the afternoon. We're seeing a lot of whitecaps now, and all of the motion has a few of the team members struggling with seasickness. If you've never experienced this sensation, it's the most helpless feeling. It's like a night back in college when you drank way too much, your head is spinning, and you're dry heaving, only instead of being drunk, you're fully aware of everything, and just wish the world would end.

The doctor is the first to hurl over the side of the boat. I've been close a few times, but try to position myself in the lower rear of the boat in order to lessen the rocking motion. I also have tape wrapped tightly around my wrists, putting pressure on key points that control the nausea triggers, or so I've been told. Still, I haven't puked yet.

Although the mask has done wonders for Martin, he's still having problems with his lips and around the eyes. Today we have him rigged up with a giant sombrero, but it keeps getting caught in the wind and waves. I try altering it with a scissors and a staple, but it just won't stay on.

We anchor for lunch and supplies at Praihna, just as an army of school kids in their white uniforms file down a large hill toward the port. They all know "Fish Man" immediately and swarm him for autographs. Chris takes advantage of the situation by dancing on the deck of the boat, flexing his wiry little muscles for the girls, and later running down through the crowd in a hockey mask and cape.

We leave in the escort boat to continue swimming while the *Cassiquiari* is still docked at the port. The scenery downstream from Praihna has changed dramatically. There are hills now in the distance, huge green mini mountains that remind me of the Mississippi River bluffs back home. The horizon is dominated by a huge, green plateau on the left side of the river that stays in view for the entire afternoon.

The wind finally abates for the last two hours before sunset. Although the wind is continuing to be a major obstacle, the current is still quite strong, and Martin is able to fight his way another forty-four miles toward Belem. The team anchors in a small inlet, fifteen miles downstream from Praihna, in an area swarming with vampire bats. Someone finds a fake bat in the movie prop bag, and we decide to play a prank on Martin. We wait until he's almost finished eating, and I lower it down from a fishing line, dangling it up and down rapidly in front of his face. He jumps back and then laughs, but the doctor is more surprised and gives us all a blood curdling scream.

March 28—Almeirim, Brazil

Although we have armed men on the boat now, there is still a concern over our safety. One precaution we're forced to make is to find a place to sleep each night near the largest possible sort of habitation. Much of the afternoons are spent on the radio with Miguel and Borut, looking at maps, and trying to project a likely place to end the day where we will be offered some sort of further protection from potential raiders.

If anything, having the armed men on board makes me even more jumpy. Back in Peru, without the armed guards, we didn't fully realize how at risk we were. Now we have men roaming the boat with automatic weapons, reminding us at all times about the risks involved each evening as we sleep. My paranoia has also worsened after hearing so many pirate stories lately. Every time I hear a critter in the wall or someone in a room above me shifting in their sleep I fear the worst, jump up in bed completely awake, and try to decide whether to hide under the bed or wield my machete. Between the bugs, heat, and paranoia, sleeping can be nearly impossible. I find myself utilizing Igor's sleeping pressure point quite often.

Martin has cut down on his wine and beer drinking after dealing with hydration issues for the first few weeks in Brazil. Still, he doesn't drink nearly enough water for a man who's exerting himself in such a way, and I'm astounded at how he manages to keep his cells replenished. I drink between ten and fifteen bottles of water each day, while he only drinks about three pints of hydration fluid while swimming, and a few glasses of juice before bed.

The river is so wide now, I find myself missing those times back in the relatively narrow parts in Peru when we could turn off the motor, paddle near the shoreline, and listen to howler monkeys and birds. Now I feel as if we're lost in this horizonless sea.

Sometimes it feels like we're not even moving, but the distant shorelines are quickly slipping past and the landmarks just keep appearing and disappearing.

With all this water moving at such an alarming rate, I have the sensation of being pulled into the Atlantic Ocean like water being sucked into a bathtub drain, and Martin is just a little bubble on the surface. I guess it's kind of accurate as major rivers are in some ways just giant drainage ditches for their respective basins.

It's getting harder and harder for our escort boat to stay with Martin. The wind knocks us around so much and we have to keep our distance so the front of the boat doesn't crash down on top of his head in the waves. Martin bullies his way through rain and large waves to swim another forty-six miles today.

Rain is limiting visibility to only a mile. Suddenly an ocean tanker appears through the haze, bearing down on us at full speed. I can communicate with the *Cassiquiari*, but don't have a way to talk to other boats, instead I rely on the *Cassiquiari* to talk to them and advise us. For whatever reason, the *Cassiquiari* can't make contact, and this monster boat heads right for us at full speed. Maybe the captain is asleep or something, or they just don't see us. I whistle to Martin, but he refuses to get on the boat, so we basically just sit there like a bunch of numbskulls, hoping it won't hit us. The vessel veers off a little to the left at the last moment, and we get thrashed hard in the wake. Slightly pissed, I speak to Miguel and Borut after the incident, and we're going to work on getting our escort boat radio equipped with new capabilities. It takes a little time for a tanker to change direction, and it's essential we're able to communicate our intentions to them, right or left, especially as we approach the ocean and run into heavier traffic.

The current here is still strong, but it's reputed to slow down considerably as the Atlantic Ocean begins to influence the Amazon River in the next ten days. Martin can expect to swim through a desolate area in the next few days, and ocean tanker traffic will continue to increase as we approach Belem. Martin refreshes himself at the end of the day with Igor's Spring of Life. I've tried the salty energy drink, and it makes me want to jump in the Amazon and swim too.

At Almeirim, as a few of us sit on the deck drinking beer, we watch several rats scurrying around the cargo boxes on the city docks. One of them gets on our anchor rope and attempts to tightrope its way onto the *Cassiquiari*, but one of the Brazilians shakes him off into the water. There have been several mouse sightings and signs of mice on the boat in the last few days. Miguel tells us that it's common for rats and mice to find ways to stow away on boats as they load up supplies in towns along the river. He says they fumigate the boat at the beginning and end of every long voyage, but the rodents find a way onboard somewhere in between.

March 29—Tapara, Brazil

Finally, we get a reprieve from the wind today. For the first time in eight days, Martin is able to use his famous crawl stroke without being pounded in the face relentlessly by waves. Martin uses 30,000 strokes in an average day of swimming. I've counted. Actually, they're more like punches. His opponent, the mighty Amazon, towers over him and surrounds him, but after fifty-seven days of taking a pounding, he's still fighting.

I haven't swam with Martin for over a week; the water's been too rough. Today is excruciatingly hot, so I get in for a few minutes after lunch. The water here is coffee-colored; you can't even see your hands in front of you. Add that to the massive width of the river, and our proximity to the ocean, and it becomes an intimidating feeling. I start thinking about bull sharks, which are definitely a possibility now, and other things that might be under the surface of the water watching my flailing legs just under the surface appetizingly. I only last a few minutes before I chicken out and get back into the boat.

Today is by far the calmest of the last few weeks, and Martin capitalizes on the favorable weather conditions and a faster-than-expected current to log forty-seven miles, his highest total in eight days. Tomorrow, he'll come to the famous fork of the Amazon, the northern route going to Macapa and the southern to Belem as the river begins to fragment into branches at the mouth before emptying into the sea.

Every night after we anchor, weathered, shirtless men in dugout canoes full of flopping fish come to sell us their daily wares, and Miguel always buys. I'm not sure if he feels sorry for them, is afraid to offend them, or if he feels they'll help keep an eye out for us if he buys from them, but he always buys at least a few fish from every canoe that approaches.

Today, however, I finally see him turn a man down. The man has a giant Paraiba that fills his entire canoe. The Paraiba is considered to be the largest freshwater fish in the Amazon, and is otherwise known as the giant, man-sized catfish of Amazonian lore. This is the first one I've seen after hearing about it for the last two months. I guess it to be about 150 pounds, roughly my size. Legends abound about these giant Paraiba swallowing babies and dogs whole. This one, I'm told, is on the small side.

We have fish for dinner again tonight. I enjoy fish, but on the Amazon, we eat fish every night. Miguel doesn't buy all these fish for nothing. They have many different ways of preparing them, but one thing is always certain: beware of bones. They don't filet the fish out here like they do back home, instead they chop off the fins with a machete, cut off the tail, take out the guts, and cook the thing whole so as not to waste a single scrap of flesh. Taking out the bones is up to the eater.

March 30—Gurupa, Brazil

Martin is blessed with ideal swimming conditions for the second day in a row, as it's cloudy, with light winds. Two quick cloudbursts of rain keep the temperature cool. Martin makes it to Gurupa by lunchtime, where he's cheered by a large mob of fans.

Martin starts swimming downstream with Armundo and me after lunch, while the *Cassiquiari* is held up getting supplies and gasoline. Just as she's about to depart, Borut and Miguel are stopped by city officials who urge them not to anchor for the night downstream from town. They warn them of a large boat that was ambushed a few weeks ago in a long narrow channel between two islands, resulting in the deaths of two of the passengers. The attack occurred approximately twelve miles downstream from Gurupa, in the vicinity where the team is planning on sleeping for the night.

Borut passes this information on to me via radio, as we're already six miles downstream from town, and I pass it onto Martin. Martin just laughs. "Hah, it's political," he tells me. "The mayor just wants us to stay in his town, or maybe there are some pretty girls on the docks and the team wants to stay and go dancing and drinking with them tonight. Believe me, Matt, it's political."

I radio back to Borut, but he's very insistent that we return in the small boat with Martin, hire some more armed guards, and continue on in the morning. Martin wants to make forty-three miles on the day before returning, but that would put us directly in the area of the rumored attack, and we don't have the *Cassiquiari* to shadow us; she's still back in Gurupa. Martin can be very stubborn, but he's also extremely unwilling to part with money, and I appeal to his frugality by telling him we can save a lot of money on gas by keeping the *Cassiquiari* docked and returning immediately, before we get any further downstream and have to waste more gas to come back against the strong current. Besides, we're five days ahead of schedule already, will only be losing an hour and a half of daylight, and won't have to return to town in the dark.

After much urging from Borut, Miguel, and me, Martin finally agrees to the safety precaution of returning upriver to Gurupa and calling it a day. He still was able to cover thirty-nine miles. The current has slowed noticeably as we approach the delta of the river, and we can expect to see influence from the Atlantic Ocean any day now.

We're told the area between here and Belem is infamous for pirate attacks. The *Cassiquiari* is an obvious target, so the team decides to hire four more armed guards who will join the expedition tomorrow, giving us a total of seven hired guns on the boat.

I take a stroll around town before dinner, find a quaint little church with the doors and windows all open, and go inside to check it out. There isn't a service, but a few older people sitting quietly in pews praying, and a handful of small children milling around. As I sit down in the back of the church to collect my thoughts, a car pulls up outside pumping loud Brazilian music. Two little girls, not over the age of four, immediately begin dancing near the altar of the church on the raised platform where the preacher stands. They both have the Mariah Carey hair flop move down, and dance a provocative dance like you'd see the scantily clad background women on an MTV video do. Four-year-old girls doing stripper dances at the altar of the church. I guess Brazil is a land of extremes.

Later that night, a few of us go out and find a discotheque. There's a dead cat outside the bathroom door, and another nearby who is shaking uncontrollably, on the verge of dying. Nobody seems to care. Still, we're having a good time, when suddenly there's a commotion at the other end of the open-air bar, like what's common any time a fight breaks out in a bar. Being stupid and being curious, a few of us run over to see. We watch a large man in a yellow shirt kicking another who's down on the ground, then pull a gun out of the front of his pants. People begin to scatter when they see the gun, and we head for the other exit as I look back to see the big man pistol-whipping the smaller man. We don't stick around long enough to see how it all ends.

March 31—Ituquara Canal, Brazil

Much of the team is relieved to see more armed men join us this morning at Gurupa. There's some grumbling about space issues, but these are some serious dudes, and it's already obvious they take their jobs of protecting us very seriously. The mess hall is converted into a hammock room after dinner and extra rations of food are brought onboard in order to accommodate them. We now have twenty-seven men living on the boat, with others coming and going. There was complaining when we had twenty-two.

Near the end of the day, we take a right into a side-cut off the main channel of the Amazon to join a series of canals that will offer Martin protection from the wind and an adequate amount of current as opposed to the bigger water on the main channel. Looking at the maps, it's amazing to see the amount of different options we have from here to reach the ocean. The delta of the river looks like a spider web on the map. There are two main routes, the northern to Macapa and the southern to Belem. The northern route is slightly shorter and officially makes the Nile the longest river in the world, but if one takes the southern route to the sea, the Amazon becomes a few miles longer than the Nile. As for flow, the Amazon dumps more water into the ocean than the next nine rivers of the world combined. The island that sits between Macapa and Belem is called Ilha de Marajo, and is twice as big as the entire country of Slovenia.

Martin has now officially entered the delta region of the Amazon, and the team will be navigating him through a dangerous maze of narrow canals for the next few days until rejoining the big water near Breves. The team is anchored at a missionary post along the Ituquara Canal, in an area known by locals as the Straights of Breves. As the *Cassiquiari* crew is securing her anchor rope in front of a settlement of small huts, there is a commotion on shore as the men of the village hurriedly go door to door, corralling up all the women between the ages of fourteen and forty, shipping them off to an undisclosed location in a small boat. "This is the most dangerous channel on the entire Amazon," Martin tells us.

We currently have men with machine guns posted on the front and back decks of the boat, scanning the surrounding water with spotlights. Martin marvels at our military presence at the end of the day as he tries to clean the mud out of his ears after swimming forty-two miles, "Hah, pirates can join us," he invites, pointing at a husky man with an automatic weapon standing guard. Much of the crew, however, is currently in their rooms with the doors locked. Personally, I know we have solid protection here on the boat, but I can't help but get a little jumpy every time I hear the hum of a motor approaching in the night, and I just hope not to be woken by gunshots.

April 1—Straights of Breves, Brazil

Although most of the team can't wait to get out of these canals, Martin prefers them. They're narrow, so he doesn't have the wind and waves to contend with, and although the current has declined, he's still clipping along at three or four miles per hour. Despite a threat from man, nature is being relatively kind to him recently. Martin tells me she's fully accepted him now. She wasn't sure at first, but now the river has accepted him completely.

Once we pass the city of Breves and hit the big water, the real struggle will commence. He'll start tasting salt and have to deal with tides. After we reenter the main river, she'll swell to as many as twelve miles in width, and that's just the southern route, the smaller of the two. Of all the rivers in the entire world, the Amazon is responsible for 14 percent of the total output of freshwater into the sea, and you can see the influence out into the ocean for nearly 120 miles.

The biggest threat to Martin's swimming in these narrow channels is the occasional commercial boat, using the same strategy as us to avoid the big water. Martin works hard to find the optimal current, and he doesn't like to be forced out of the best current to get out of a boat's way. At times, a game of chicken ensues between us and the big boats. They radio to us and tell us to move out of the way. We radio back and tell them we have a swimmer in the water and can't move out of the way. Eventually, they maneuver in order to miss us, but they're usually not too happy about it. We've already had a few such instances, the latest occurring this afternoon. I whistled for Martin to be ready to get on the boat as a barge was heading straight for us. He shooed me away and held his ground as the boat swerved around us at the last moment. The first few close calls with commercial boats were scary, but after awhile we got bolder, figuring the added time and energy it takes him to swim out of the boat's path is too great a sacrifice for the miniscule chance the boat might actually hit us. I reserve the safety whistle as a last resort, and Martin often has angry boats whizzing around him flipping us the bird, even though he's still swimming in a straight line and not even aware they're there.

It's been several days since the wind has dropped down to a point where I'm able to have Armundo cut the motor so I can paddle the boat and keep up with Martin. These are peaceful times for Martin as we listen to the jungle finally after the noise of that annoying motor is eliminated, but it looks as if they may be a thing of the past. Martin always shows people more respect when he sees them toiling away, and he hates to see people sitting around drinking or laughing or having fun, so I try to work as much as possible around him, whether it's paddling or furiously typing on the computer at the end of the day. I've gotten into the habit of grabbing a computer and hurrying off somewhere whenever I see him, or opening it up and starting to type away, more for show than anything else. I'm always ready to put down my beer and put on a good acting job for him so he thinks I'm busting my ass a bit on this expedition. Hey, I didn't make it through three of these things for nothing.

Martin has always been a very stoic guy. He never complains, and it's nearly impossible to see how much pain he's actually feeling. I can tell he's in rough shape today when he's unable to pull himself into the boat at the end of the swimming, something he'd done every day on his own for the last two months. For me, it's like watching a person who notices for the first time they're diminishing physically due to old age. I offer him a hand, but he refuses. Only after he fails to get into the boat for a second time do Borut and I each hook an arm under his armpits and hoist him up into the boat. A long silence ensues, in which Martin sits on the floor of the boat shaking his head.

We plan on stopping a few miles upstream at a small village, but he refuses to stop until he hit his sixty-fifth kilometer. I think he's surviving purely on adrenaline at this point, and although the team has been pleading with him to conserve his energy, he's pushing forward toward the ocean at an insane rate. At this point, he's not only concerned with swimming the Amazon, but has become fixated at how many days it takes him. He barely touches his food or says a word at dinner, then quickly retires to his room. Every muscle in his body is cramping at night, especially his legs, probably from chronic dehydration, and he's only been sleeping two to three hours per night. I've been with Martin for three expeditions, and I've seen him exhausted like this, but it usually progresses more slowly. This time, it's as if it came out of nowhere. Borut and I were just talking two days ago about how strong he still was at this stage of the swim as compared to other expeditions.

Martin expects to reach Breves tomorrow, after which he'll leave the Straights of Breves and reenter the main river, which will be as many as twelve miles wide with huge waves and Oceanic tidal influences. He's still projected to reach Belem on Saturday, April 7th.

April 2—Breves, Brazil

Martin and the team spend the morning navigating through the labyrinth of channels known as the Straights of Breves. The current is actually a tad stronger than we anticipated, but Martin's progress is terrible as he's far from full power. We originally expected to reach Breves by lunchtime, but 1:00 came and went and we were still seven miles away.

Our soldier in the boat with the machine gun gets real jumpy today when a muscular, serious-faced boy of about sixteen paddles to us in a canoe, looks us over, then quickly paddles back into the woods and blows a whistle, at which point four other canoes come out of the flooded forest about a mile downstream from us. The soldier in the boat quickly scans them with our binocs and says something frantic in Portuguese. I radio the *Cassiquiari* to tell them that something is going on, and tell Martin to get ready to jump in the boat at any moment. The big boat comes in close and our soldiers all display themselves prominently. As soon as they see the armed men, all four canoes disappear back into the jungle.

By 2:00 in the afternoon the current has slowed to a trickle, and we're only progressing about one mile per hour. "Not possible," Martin tells me, "Must go more left." I can clearly see from my perched perspective atop the deck, the debris on the left shore isn't moving downstream either, but he doesn't believe me and makes a beeline for the left bank. When we get there, the current has dropped to one and a half kilometers per hour. "Must go right," he declares and starts swimming straight out for the other bank. By the time we get to the right bank, the current has stopped completely, and after ten minutes we start to move backwards; it's the tide.

I've been looking at the same island for three hours now as

Martin zigzags back and forth without covering any distance. He's wasting his energy for nothing, and it doesn't make any sense. He's swimming as hard as he can and making about half a mile per hour, then moving backwards as he stops to take a drink. I can't get him to stop. We've been directly in front of a dilapidated building with the name, "Porto Boa Vista," for the last hour. Why not just wait for the tide and use it to our advantage? I'm starting to worry that he's beginning to crack mentally.

I radio for Borut, who eventually comes out in a smaller boat to see what's wrong and to try to convince Martin to stop swimming. He's already completely spent from swimming all day, but relentless in his goal, he continues to swim against the tide, obsessed with making it to the town. We spend ten minutes trying to convince him to call it a day and conserve his energy for tomorrow, and it's not until he stops swimming, looks at the shoreline, and sees himself floating upstream toward Peru that he throws up his hands in frustration and quits for the day. Martin didn't expect to experience ocean tides until he exited the Straights of Breves.

Martin only covers twenty-seven miles on the day due to a combination of exhaustion, delirium, and tidal influences. He intended to anchor at Breves for lunch, but ends the day three miles short of the town. Martin is in even worse shape today than he was yesterday, physically exhausted, and mentally frustrated from the tides. He's not hydrating himself properly, unable to sleep, and acting irrationally.

At dinner, Borut and I talk about strategies to help deal with the wind and waves on the big water we'll face the next day. "I can stop the wind," Martin tells us. "Do you want it to rain? I can make it rain." He says it in a joking way, but then just kind of sits there, staring away blankly, not eating or drinking anything. We know the doctor has been keeping his conditions secret from us and is threatened by Igor or any other outside influences, but Martin doesn't seem to be very healthy.

We're so concerned about him after dinner that Borut and I try to sneak him into a hospital without the doctor knowing so he can get hydrated with an IV, something that worked for him on the Yangtze. We make it into the taxi and get as far as the lobby of the emergency room, Martin putting one foot in front of the other with his head down as Borut and I lead him along by his elbows. He's still in a daze as we enter the hospital, having to move out of the way as a man with a serious head wound is carried past us. The combination of all the sick people, the thought of being stuck with needles, and the chance they'd try to prevent him from swimming snaps Martin out of his delirium, because as soon as they throw the blood pressure cuff on and Borut starts filling out paperwork, his demeanor changes. He stands up, refuses treatment, and demands we leave immediately.

Borut acquires some tidal charts and tries to convince Martin only to swim during the six hour window in which the tide is going out. Martin seems to be lucid again, and plans on swimming at the normal time tomorrow.

Two angelic-looking little girls come up in a dugout canoe to beg for food, sisters, one about seven, the other nine. We give them some cookies and two shirts, and they tell us, with Miguel interpreting, that the smaller of the two was playing on the edge of the water when a giant anaconda came and coiled around her. She was so tiny and the Anaconda was so huge that it was unable to squeeze her to death because there was too much space between the coils. Her brave older sister crept in, grabbed the little girl by the hair and pulled her out, and they both escaped. Many people of the village consider the little girl to be divine since the incident. We hear a lot of stories like this on the river and never know how much is true.

These little jungle kids are so much more adaptable than their counterparts to the far north. American kids might be able to burn DVDs, save the princess in the latest video game, and tell you if your shoes are cool or not, but the true jungle child beams you right in the eyes with an uncontaminated, spirit-tingling, unflinching gaze as you interrupt them chopping the fins off a bottom feeding fish from a squatting, bent-knee position in a small gap in the shrubbery on the river's edge.

April 3—Bagre, Brazil

After a rough night, Martin gets back into the water at 7:00 this morning as the tides are swelling to their highest level and are just about to start receding again. The doctor comes with us on the escort boat, administering psychotherapy to him as he swims on his back. Martin is a strong, silent man, but in every expedition he's found someone to confide in about his problems at the end of each day. She seems to help balance him out when she administers cognitive therapy to him, and just having a woman to talk to on a boat full of men helps too. They speak in Slovenian while he does the backstroke so I don't know what they're talking about, but they talk for a solid hour, and he seems to be coming back to reality again.

The day is remarkably calm. We make it to the big water, and it's like glass, one of those days you only get on the water about once or twice per summer when everything seems perfect. Maybe Martin stopped the wind? Igor's wife, Irma joins us for the day; perhaps they did it. If only they could do something about the tide.

Martin is still in the habit of picking up floating flowers or other pieces of jungle foliage, examining them, and sometimes keeping them in one hand as he swims on his back for up to an hour at a time. I can't help but think of Frankenstein when I see such tender moments from such a gruff-looking man.

Martin goes back to doing the crawl stroke while I talk to the doctor. She informs me that over the course of the last week, he's been suffering from cramps, dangerously high blood pressure, chronic insomnia, and a coetaneous larvae infection, all of which he's stoically kept hidden from us.

The current is strong up until about 2:00, at which time the tide turns and progress slows considerably. By 4:30, he's only making one mile per hour. When the tide is at its lowest level, Martin suddenly stops swimming and stands up in the middle of a body of water that is nearly twelve miles wide and begins laughing. The *Cassiquiari* is beached for ten minutes but comes loose when the tide starts rising again.

When things have gotten tough for Martin in past expeditions, Borut, a competitive swimmer for many years, has jumped into the water to swim with his father and offer him some silent encouragement. He usually reserves these moments for times when he can see his father is running out of steam.

Borut is swimming with Martin today when out of the blue he stands and shows us he too can walk in the shallow water. Suddenly he yells out in pain and lifts his right foot. I can't see anything at first, but when we get him into the small boat, blood is coming out from a small puncture wound in his heel and he's in a great deal of pain. The doctor stops the bleeding and Miguel later tells us that Borut had been hit by a stingray, very common in this area. Borut suffers through a very uncomfortable afternoon, limping around the boat and grunting a lot. We make a decision to avoid the shallow sand flats when the tide is dropping.

Martin finally calls it quits for the day when he starts moving backward an hour later. Although it's a beautiful day, Martin is frustrated after a tough day of swimming in which he struggled forward only another twenty-nine miles. "I can't sleep anyway, I might as well just swim at night," Martin tells us at dinner. Although much of the team tries to dissuade him because of the obvious dangers involved, Martin has a good point. We only have two six hour windows of optimal tide per day, one at approximately 8:00 in the morning, and the other at about 8:00 at night.

We have a meeting to discuss the logistics of night swimming, and although I am against it, both Martin and Borut agree it would be a good idea to use the tides and lack of winds to our favor. We prepare to go out, but a strong storm blows in and makes us cancel our plans. I'm relieved. Martin's very tired already, we're ahead of schedule, and there's no reason to push any more.

April 4—Curralinho, Brazil

Martin starts swimming at the normal time again this morning. Valter radios in to tell us he's swimming strongly and the tides are favorable. For the last few days, every time we anchor we're approached by dugout canoes full of children, or at times, entire families. They're very poor and just want us to throw them down a few scraps of food or some clothes, anything. The little kids look like heavenly creatures to me, 100 percent pure. Their faces are so earnest and their eyes so thoughtful, I can't even return their gazes. I feel guilty for having nothing to give, and if I gave a shirt or something to one, the rest of them would be left out.

We're seeing more houses today. They're all up on stilts due to the tidal influences. There are no roads or connecting paths between the houses, and everyone travels everywhere by canoe. The children are all expert canoeists at an early age. There is no playground; they get together in their canoes and play.

Martin takes only a ten-minute lunch today, telling us, "We have to eat fast." He quickly scarfs down his food, yells, "Let's go," and jumps back in the river before the tides change. He seems to be in much better shape than either of the previous two days. I'm quite sure that the fact he's finally chosen to work with the tides rather than against them has made things much easier for him. He tells us he can taste salt now and it makes him happy after swimming for sixty-three days to finally sense the nearness of the ocean.

I turn my ankle pretty bad trying to jump from one moving boat to another and am having a hard time putting weight on it. The doctor is busy going over Martin, so I turn to the natural healers. Irma and Igor get together and tape a penny over my belly button. "The problem is in your colon," Irma tells me. "This will also help to keep your spiritual energy from escaping. It's an ancient technique used by Hippocrates." Irma then forces her thumb up and under the gap below my breast bone, making me scream out in pain. She holds it there for a full three seconds, explaining she has to release energy from my head to help it move down and heal the foot. The last thing she does is to massage the other foot in order to force energy up and over my hips and back down for the injured foot to borrow.

The doctor soon appears, angry at me for taking the treatments of the spiritualists. I figure I'll take whatever I can get, and later get some strong painkillers from her. I feel better after an hour, and am not sure whom to attribute the healing to.

I feel like we're on the longest straightway on the world's biggest horseracing track. At times we can barely see the horizon in three of the four directions, and when we do see land, it's usually just another giant island. Many people on the boat are starting to snap. It's always the first few days and the last few days of a long expedition that are the most difficult, and years later it's only the first and last days that I can remember clearly, the rest is just a giant blur. We've had a lot of tension lately on the boat as people are psychologically wasted from living on a boat together for so long. Some of us on the boat are barely holding it together, and things we didn't say a month ago are all coming out now in the final days.

The doctor does many things to help Martin, both physically and mentally, but she's became active in every aspect of the expedition, at times undermining Borut's authority as expedition leader. In addition, she's kept many of Martin's ailments from the camera crew, and they're upset with her because they feel as if Martin's suffering is something that should be documented as part of the film. After I make the mistake of sharing with John some details of an earlier conversation with the doctor in which she revealed some of Martin's ailments, he makes a beeline to her room and unleashes a flurry of frustration for keeping it a from the documentary. He's especially angry that she insists on speaking to Martin in Slovene, thus nullifying any attempt for his crew to capture the dialogue.

Martin is only able to swim twenty-four miles today until the waves and tides beat him into submission before he reaches the daily goal of Curralinho. He's determined to finish the swim on Saturday, and the only way to do so is to utilize both tidal windows each day. This means swimming at night.

Although I am completely against the idea, we prepare for night swimming after dinner. We dock in Curralinho for safety, and Borut, Martin, and I go upstream six miles from town to where we left off that afternoon. The ride itself is frightening. We're all soaked from breaking through the waves, have close calls with boats running without lights and an island, and I'm worried about being pirated. There is a silent tension on the boat that shows in the faces of all of us onboard, like men going off to do battle. Martin has decided we don't need the soldiers for such a short distance, and we only have one lifejacket on the boat, two facts that do little to please me. It takes me half an hour to come to terms with the situation. I'm not angry, I'm not scared; I'm numb, completely resigned to whatever unpredictability the night will bring. What we're doing is dangerous, it's stupid, but hey, so is swimming down the Amazon in the first place. We're here, and we have to finish the job.

Martin jumps in and immediately begins swimming in the wrong direction; it's extremely difficult to gauge where we are and where we need to go. Although we begin with a spotlight, he's afraid the beam will attract large predators such as bull sharks, or draw other unwanted attention, so we tie a glowing red neon stick to the back of his wetsuit, wait until our eyes adjust to the darkness, and use the speckles of light coming from the moon as our reference point. A few large boats temporarily blind us with their spotlights, but we're able to make radio contact and ask in broken Portuguese for their cooperation.

It's mesmerizing watching the little red neon stick that is Martin Strel appear and disappear in the darkness. Occasionally, voices from anchored boats carry over to us from miles away. We do our best to hold a straight line while staying far enough from Martin not to run him over, but close enough not to lose him and to throw a rescue line if trouble should come. It's pins and needles all night.

Although confusing and dangerous, the night is a success as Martin is able to capitalize on the outgoing tides to make another seven miles toward his goal, which now lays only sixty-seven miles away. We're all counting down now. He makes it out of the boat under his own power, but the tired swimmer slips and falls off a plank getting back onto the *Cassiquiari*, suffering small cuts and abrasions in several places on his legs, arms, and torso.

April 5—São Francisco, Brazil

So far on this journey down the most dangerous river in the world, the Amazon has been very accepting of Martin, keeping him safe from dangerous predators, pirates, and tropical diseases. One of his biggest fears for this final stage of the trip is of the Pororoca, a huge tidal bore that occurs where incoming tides meet the outflow of the Amazon. They've been recorded to reach heights of thirty feet, speeds of twenty-four miles per hour, and reach as far inland as sixty miles, destroying everything in their path, including large boats. The Pororoca has become legendary amongst the top surfers of the world, and many have lost their lives attempting to ride it. The phenomenon is possible whenever lunar and solar tides synchronize, but according to meteorological experts, no Pororocas have been forecast from now until Sunday . . . although you never know. We're examining the possibilities of taking a slightly longer route along a side channel to Belem in order avoid the big water.

I've basically become the night man now as Valter navigates the mornings; the afternoons are shot because of the tides. We keep close radio contact with Martin via Valter, but Valter has become so overprotective of Martin's privacy and stoicism that, like the doctor, he never truly reveals how bad a shape Martin is in. Although I've become the first non-Slovene to penetrate Martin's inner circle, I'm not Slovenian, and the other Slovenes on the boat with the exception of Borut still have ways to keep me away from him. Borut and I have become extremely tight on this expedition. We have serious conversations about logistics every evening, and although he prefers to handle everything himself, I've convinced him to delegate a few of his more minor responsibilities to me.

Martin battles the waves and tides with Valter to move another twenty-two miles toward his goal today. He appears to be lucid and in pretty good shape when I see him briefly at the lunch table before he retires to his room. He tells us he plans to brave the moonlit waters of the Amazon again the next two evenings in order to make it to the finish line in time. He's only forty-four miles from the end now, but moving along at a snail's pace.

After thinking his exhaustion and bout with delirium was over a few days ago, Martin takes a serious turn for the worse a few hours after swimming today. He seems fine when he comes out of the water, but at 4:00 he staggers out of his room using the wall to help hold himself up and asks someone to get the doctor. He complains of dizziness and seems to have a hard time standing. The doctor examines him, finding his blood pressure to be jumping off the charts. He also has vertigo, diarrhea, nausea, and his stomach is extremely bloated, noticeably sticking way out like a sick Ethiopian kid on an infomercial.

He can barely stand on his own power, but it's a beautiful calm evening with a nearly full moon, a perfect night for swimming. The doctor is nearly in tears as she begs him not to go, but Martin insists on going back out on the river at 8:00 PM. She comes with us on the escort boat, warning Borut and I that if he starts vomiting while swimming it could mean instant death. I hold a rescue line for the duration of the evening. We also bring an armed soldier and find one more life jacket.

The night is beautiful. The winds are light, and the almost-full moon comes in and out of shrouds of clouds, filtering purplish light out over the rippling waters. We do the majority of the swim without the aid of any light. We watch as Martin's glowing red neon marker zigzags back and forth constantly. He can't hold a straight line nor stay with the escort boat. We try to point out the proper direction to swim and he doesn't believe us, instead choosing to go his own way. Once he lets out a tirade of swear-words at Borut, who is just trying to point him downstream. We nearly collide with an anchored boat and hear vulgar Portuguese bouncing across the water at us. We ask if he's ready to stop every half mile, but he just keeps swimming. He makes seven miles over nearly three hours before he finally takes the doctor's advice and quits for the night. "I've had enough. I just want to finish and go home," he tells us. He has a strange, almost confused look in his eyes.

Borut and I have to pull him back into the boat. I've had to help get Martin out of the water before, but this time, we literally pull him out of the water. It reminds me of an old dog I had that took a swim in the lake every day and tried to catch a goose. They'd all fly off, and then he'd jump out of the water and shake off, like dogs do. One day he was physically unable to pull himself out of the lake, and my Dad and I had to assist him. The confused look in his eyes was the same one I see in Martin's. My dog learned quickly not to jump back into the water, instead he'd hobble around on the bank and the geese would follow him around curiously and he'd look out at them sadly, knowing he was physically unable to join them. Martin, on the other hand, just gets back into the water even though he knows he's physically unable to get out.

He lies down on the dirty floor of the boat and falls asleep as we drive back to the *Cassiquiari*. We wake him up when we arrive. He's confused and physically unable to walk under his own power, so Borut and I hook an arm under each of his shoulders and guide him straight to his room. He feels like a limp, drunk man, and I am nervous about getting puked on. He starts mumbling something in Slovene to Borut as we unzip his wetsuit and help him out of his clothes. His entire body is slimy and smells terribly. Stripping his socks off is one of the worst smelling things I've ever encountered. He soon shoos us away, lies down in his wet underwear, and immediately passes out. I bring a bucket into his room and lay it next to his bed.

April 6—Ponta de Pedras, Brazil

By the time I wake up, Martin is gone, having left with Valter at 7:00 in the morning. The doctor is talking to Borut in Slovene in a very serious, concerned manner, and I suspect Martin went out against her advice. The tide is nearing its lowest level now, and the dock that we'd stepped onto so easily before is now ten feet above our heads.

I express my worries to Borut, but he reminds me of previous swims in which Martin had similar symptoms and kept swimming. We only have two days and thirty-seven miles remaining. Still, we decide to postpone our arrival into Belem one day.

We've been very fortunate with the weather since we hit the big water. Martin still thinks he's been able to influence the winds. "See how calm. The river here is never calm. The Amazon stays calm for me." He also tells us that the animals of the river have accepted him, and he no longer feels any worries about piranha, anaconda, candirú, crocodiles, or other predators. He's even taken to removing his wetsuit on particularly hot afternoons from time to time. Maybe it's true. Maybe he can communicate directly with the river. He's fully enveloped by it at all times, either physically surrounded in the water, or mentally as he stares into the wall in his room each night and prepares for the next day.

We live in a world where we're pulled this way and that on a daily basis by things that are so small and meaningless, yet at the time they seem to rule our entire existence. In effect, we're slaves to our house payments, the price of gasoline, microwave ovens and cable television. As I've watched Martin's struggle against the river for the last few days, I've come to realize that for him, those mundane things no longer exist. It's just Martin and the river, nothing else. He's eliminated every aspect of the entire universe and it's now just him and the creatures of the Amazon—his brothers from the muddy water.

Because the tides are favorable in the mornings, I've had a lot of time on my hands as Martin spends the afternoons resting. Valter informs me that Martin oozed forward another nineteen miles over the course of about seven hours of swimming, ending at approximately 2:00 for lunch. He swam on his back for a good portion of the day, an obvious sign of his exhaustion. At this point he swims for six or seven hours, tries to rest for six hours, then goes out at night to add a few more to his daily total. I accompany him at night, and although it's only for a few hours, I still disagree with Borut over the need to swim at night. Martin is so worried about making it to Belem in time to please the media for a big reception that he's pushing himself way too hard, and making decisions, like night swimming, that put the entire team in jeopardy. I've told Borut that as expedition leader, he needs to put a stop to such nonsense, but Martin is his dad, and no matter what the job title is on the expedition, the father will always be in charge. Maybe that's why Martin chose his son as expedition leader.

Martin is still having stomach problems, but insists on night swimming again tonight, once again going against doctor's orders. His blood pressure is abnormally high, and his delirium is also obvious. Martin is a total numbers freak. He always knows exactly how many kilometers he's swum, and how many he has left. Tonight, as we prepare for night swimming, Martin puts his hand on my shoulder and says wearily, "Matthew, how many kilometers left to swim? Less than one hundred?" Actually we're only twenty-nine kilometers away from the goal at this point, and we've been talking about the number of kilometers from the finish line constantly since we were 120 away. Martin always knows exactly how far he is from both the starting and ending point of a river, so for me this is an obvious red flag, and I inform the doctor. She insists on going with us again for night swimming in order to monitor him.

Night swimming goes terribly. Martin is in a foul mood, screaming at Borut that there are too many people in the boat. He doesn't want the doctor monitoring him, and he says there is no need for the soldier to stand guard. It's a very dark night as the moon and stars are covered with sinister looking clouds; a light rain comes and goes. We need to use lights to see where we're going, but every time we turn on the spotlight to attempt to get a visual, Martin stops swimming and unleashes a flurry of swearwords at Borut and me. We cross paths dangerously close to vessels heading upstream twice, the second time blinding us all with its light. Martin admits he's feeling ill, which we know means he's extremely ill, so after making only three miles in two hours, Borut and I finally convince him to call it quits. Again we have to assist him into his room, but he's much more lucid than the night before. We end the evening only fourteen miles from our destination.

April 7—Ponta de Pedras

Martin begins swimming today a little earlier as the tidal windows have been changing as we approach the ocean. For all practical purposes, we're in the ocean now. Martin is currently swimming at a line of latitude almost even with Belem, but he's actually on the other side of the river from Belem. The river is over nine miles wide, and the island to our left, Marajo, is half the size of Iowa.

To name an exact location where a river meets the sea is completely nominal. Deltas continue to move outward as sediment is transferred further and further out to sea. As an example, most people believe the Mississippi River ends at New Orleans. In actuality, the point called mile zero, which again is nominal, occurs more than ninety miles from the city. Our official ending point is just an imaginary straight line of latitude from the mouth of the Rio Capim, where Belem is located, across from Ponta De Pedras.

The doctor tells us Martin's nausea and diarrhea have subsided, but he's still dizzy and needs someone to help him with walking when he gets out of the water. Strangely, he tells us he doesn't experience the vertigo when swimming, only on land. My guess is that it has something to do with having his body tossed to and fro in the waves for so long.

Those of us on the *Cassiquiari* follow Martin's escort boat, all of us with our eyes completely fixated on our three GPSs counting down the kilometers to the official ending point. We're only a few kilometers from the end, but it all seem so anticlimactic, partially because there isn't an actual finish line, just a GPS marking. Back on the Mississippi, Martin had to physically touch a big stone beacon that said mile zero.

We're staying near the shore to offer some wind protection, so Borut and I decide to go ahead to the ending point in another boat to put up a few banners and some flags at the exact line of latitude marking the end of the swim. Within a few feet of the line we find a small, hut-like dwelling where three shirtless kids happily play in the water, oblivious to a lightly falling rain. A green pet parrot sits silently on a small tree limb near the hut, and their father and mother peek out the window suspiciously as we set up the banners across some palm trees in their muddy yard.

Martin endures the final six hours of suffering in total silence, stopping only a few times to motion for a drink. His pace is faster than we've seen in several days, but the contorted features of his face show his pain as he points his lips skyward to gasp for air with each stroke. I can actually hear him drawing oxygen into his lungs each time he looks skyward, a phenomenon I've never witnessed with Martin.

The rain has picked up now, the wind increases, and large waves batter the swimmer. I can tell he's swallowing a lot of water, occasionally spitting some out as he comes up for another breath, yet he swims the final fourteen miles with unwavering determination.

Martin crosses the finish line, crawls up the muddy bank on his hands and knees, and touches our ramshackle series of banners and flags at approximately 12:30 in the afternoon. With tears in his eyes and a quivering jaw, he fights hard to keep his emotions from showing.

After stopping long enough to take a few pictures at the ending point, Martin gets back into his small escort boat, motors back upstream to the anchored *Cassiquiari*, has a bowl of soup, and goes into his room. There are a few pats on the back, a half-assed toast, and some hugs, but no speeches, no laughter, and no out-ward emotion. Martin is physically spent and although he seems as though mentally he's not even aware that he just became the first man in the history of the world to swim the Amazon, I know he's in his room right now with his eyes closed but not asleep, going over the trip in his mind. Blistering images of the last sixty-six days dance through his entire being, causing him to undulate between tears and laughter, and he doesn't want us all to see that. Plus, he's just too exhausted to celebrate. He knows he still has to do a promotional swim into Belem tomorrow, so for him the swim is still not completely over.

The entire team is mentally wasted, and to a man, I don't think any of us understand the significance of what just occurred. The unofficial Guinness totals were 5,268 kilometers swam over the course of sixty-six days.

Tomorrow he'll take a side chute off the Amazon and swim with the incoming tides up the Rio Capim to reach the legendary city of Belem, the first center of Portuguese colonization along the Amazon. Tomorrow's swim is basically just to greet the media. Officially, Martin is finished. He plans to arrive at Estacao Das Docas at 11:00 AM.

While Martin is in his room being tended to by the doctor, a bunch of us go into a seedy portside bar to celebrate. We decide to shoot a game of pool and find a frightened three-toed sloth tied to the pool table in the opposite corner of the bar. The poor thing is shaking all over, has abrasions in many places and appears to be completely petrified. I'll never forget the sad look of resignation and distrust in its eyes. Some of the locals in the bar try to feed it a bowl of beer, forcing its head into the bowl when it refuses to drink on its own accord. I can only imagine what kinds of terrors the sloth has experienced at the hands of different groups of rough-neck sailors who come into the bar from port and mistreat the poor thing for their amusement.

We learn from the owner of the bar using our own combined broken Portuguese and some pantomiming that his teenage son and a few friends found the slow-moving sloth low in a tree on the edge of the town, tore it off the tree with considerable effort and brought it into the bar about a week ago. The man and his family are planning on eating it for Easter Sunday dinner tomorrow.

After a long negotiation process in which we're prepared to pay as much as fifty dollars, we buy the tormented animal for five dollars and release it into its natural jungle habitat. Getting the thing out of the bar and into Martin's escort boat was easy, but when we arrive at some high ground on a nearby island, the sloth, which we refer to as "Eight Ball," has a death grip on the floor of the boat with all four of his three-clawed arms and legs. We have to take the entire floor of the boat out with the sloth attached and carry it into the jungle. We find a huge tree that spreads out in many directions with large branches and many leaves, lean the floor board of the boat up against it, step back, and watch as Eight Ball slowly releases his death grip and begins to inch his way up the tree in slow motion.

It takes about half an hour for Eight Ball to make it to a place near the top of the tree, where he slowly turns himself upside down, grabs a claw full of leaves and begins to eat. Confident he'll be safe in his new home, we walk back to the boat silently, some of us with tears in our eyes, but all of us with a happy feeling in our hearts.

What a day. Martin swam the Amazon, and we saved a sloth. I fall asleep with a split-screened brain, Martin and the Sloth. I dream the two are coming together, Martin is tied to the pool table, the pool table becomes the Amazon and Martin is swimming in slow motion toward shore. He crawls onto the muddy bank slowly climbs to the top of a large Lupuna tree where he'll live forever, happily eating twigs and leaves. He's free now.

April 8—Belem, Brazil

The last day of the expedition is supposed to be a promotional swim into the city of Belem to greet the media. It becomes much more than that. Many local media boats discover our location approximately six miles from Belem, and try to board our boat to interview Martin. Our satellite phones are ringing off the hook with CNN, BBC, ABC, NBC, etcetera, basically every major news source in the world, calling at once wanting to talk to Martin. I help Borut filter the media, only talking to the largest outlets in the world. Meanwhile, we still have to get a mentally and physically exhausted swimmer prepared for swimming into the city of Belem.

Amidst all the chaos and confusion of being bombarded by phone calls from world media, the ever changing emotions of all of us involved as the expedition comes to a close, and trying to keep local media off the boat, Martin is extremely tense. Suddenly he surprises us all, well before we're scheduled to start for the day, and hollers, "Let's go."

Valter can't locate the magnetic pen for the stupid board, and Martin goes crazy about this. He has six people on board the escort boat taking out the floorboards, scouring the entire boat for the magnetic pen, but nobody can locate it. Media boats constantly criss-cross in front of us at an unsafe distance, and Martin, can smell their exhaust fumes under the water. He pops his head up and screams at Valter in Slovene to make them leave while motioning wildly with his right hand to wave them out of his path.

He covers the first mile through a narrow canal with relative ease, but when the canal opens up into the big water and the skyline of Belem appears on the horizon, our progress comes nearly to a halt. The tides aren't pulling us toward Belem, they're taking us away from the city, out toward the ocean. Between Borut, Martin, and me, we collectively misinterpreted the oceanic tidal charts as to how they relate to the Rio Capim during all the confusion of the last day. We now have a major problem on our hands. There are media boats everywhere, we have thousands of people and a camera for every major media outlet waiting for us on shore, nearly within view, Martin is completely exhausted, and we're being pushed away from the city, out toward the Atlantic Ocean.

Martin's anger at this is unfathomable. The day was supposed to be an easy little swim to wave hello to the media, raise his arms in victory, and celebrate his accomplishment. Instead, he has to swim the final few kilometers against the current. The smart thing to do would be to wait a few hours for the tide to change, but there are too many people waiting on shore, and we're only about two and a half miles from the destination. Martin decides to hunker down and give it his all in the last leg of what may be the last swim of his career.

The day is remarkably calm, and he is able to swim exclusively using the crawl stroke. The problem is that we can't keep him in a straight line. He keeps angling further and further to the left, until at one point he's moving directly away from his destination of Das Docas. I blow the whistle at him several times and point the proper way for him, and he throws up his hands and says something in Slovene. I'm not sure what he said because Borut just shakes his head and says it doesn't make any sense. After continuously tooting on the whistle and pointing him in the right direction toward a large building he needs to swim toward, Martin finally starts to hold a relatively straight line.

He may not know exactly where he is, but knows he has to keep swimming. In what was supposed to be a promotional swim to greet the media in Belem, Martin is struggling more at this moment than at any time during the entire expedition. He gives it his all, but is only closing the gap at a rate of a little more than a mile per hour. He's no longer swimming hands over shoulders like an overhand baseball pitcher; his arms are flailing side-armed, nearly parallel to the water. He can't get them up above his head anymore and is making inefficient splashes as he fights his way forward like a heavyweight fighter in the twelfth round who needs a knockout to win.

After more than three hours of what was supposed to be just over a one hour swim, we can finally see the people on shore waiting to receive Martin. He's still throwing punches, but the clumsiness of his strokes and failure to hold a straight line reveal his complete and total exhaustion.

Borut suggests I go forward in another small boat in order to find the exact location where Martin needs to land and radio back the information to him. I can't find any place very suitable, but decide upon a small yellow ladder along a retaining wall in the center of a throng of people.

I watch as Martin and the escort boat zigzag their way toward us in slow-motion. By the time Martin sees the crowd of people and tries to acknowledge their cheers with a wave, it looks to me like he's having a hard time staying above water; he looks as though he's practically drowning.

It takes three of us using all of our strength to hoist Martin's limp fish body up and over the retaining wall. He cannot stand on his own two feet and is fighting to regain his breath. Luckily, some paramedics are standing by and we help him into a wheelchair where they promptly strap on an oxygen mask. A mob of excited people crowds around Martin and he lifts a hand in a feeble wave of acknowledgment, but for the most part is oblivious to their presence.

Amidst all the pandemonium, Martin is whisked away by the paramedics who insist he be hospitalized. We fight our way through the crowd of several thousand people to arrive at an ambulance. Borut has disappeared in the crowd of people at some point between the dock and the ambulance, so I help transfer Martin's deadweight body from the wheelchair to a gurney, and we lift him up and into the back of the vehicle. The paramedics beckon me to crawl inside with him, and we can barely get the doors closed as the crowd continues to swarm.

He still hasn't spoken or barely moved, but after twenty minutes in the ambulance, with an IV and some oxygen, he starts to come to his senses a bit. His eyes water over, he takes off the oxygen mask to speak and asks me in a soft, low voice, "Borut, Borut, where's Borut?" I use my radio to call and discover Borut is right outside the backdoor of the ambulance, but the security guards don't believe he's Martin's son and won't let him in. The entire ambulance is surrounded by media, all trying to get the security guards to let them open a door to snap off a quick photo of Martin. We struggle to get the doors open, let Borut inside and then reclose the doors. Borut is emotional at the sight of his father hooked up to machines in the ambulance. He immediately takes his hand, and both men struggle to hold back their tears.

As soon as Borut gets inside the ambulance, Martin immediately becomes more lucid. We drive to the hospital, but Martin refuses to go inside, insisting he have his personal doctors treat him. Against the objections of the paramedics, we take him to a hotel, wheel him into his room on a stretcher, and wait for Doctors de Leonni Stanonik and Latifi to arrive. The paramedics refuse to leave until the doctors are present, and it takes about half an hour before they finally call our room from the lobby. Borut and I reluctantly leave as the doctors begin hooking Martin to an assortment of monitoring machines they'd wheeled in.

April 12—Belem, Brazil

After spending four days resting and being closely monitored by the doctors, Martin is back on his feet again. Although he lost a total of thirty-six pounds during the swim, his heart rate is back to normal, and his blood pressure is getting better. The doctors tell us he's actually in great shape for a fifty-two year old man who'd just spent the last ten weeks swimming the Amazon.

Martin and the team are all now entering that tough stage of mental exhaustion that stems from the transition between expedition life and returning to reality. I can't believe it's over, it all feels like a dream. The entire trip blurs through my mind as I lay around in my room all day, hoping to catch the latest clip of Martin on CNN. I sleep a lot, forget to eat, and scarcely believe I was a part of this incredible endeavor. Four days have passed since Martin reached Belem, but I really can't remember anything from those days.

Martin is keeping a low profile also. His room is directly below mine and I stop in occasionally to say hello and see if he needs anything, but he's usually in there alone, laying in bed and staring out the window with soft, contemplative eyes, swimming through the images in his mind and undoubtedly trying to figure out what the heck he's going to do next.

EPILOGUE

Martin Strel is a little fat. Martin Strel is a little old. Martin Strel likes to drink a little beer and wine. When Martin Strel walks around in his Speedo, some people actually laugh. "Where's the swimmer?" they ask. What those doubters don't understand is that the moment Martin Strel changes into his wetsuit, he changes from a slightly old, slightly fat man into a superhero. He sits in his room gazing out the window, conjuring up visions of big rivers, then slips on a Speedo, pulls his wetsuit over the top, makes his way across the globe to the start of that river, and jumps in.

There are millions of people throughout the world gazing out that same window. Occasionally a crazy thought comes into their head from somewhere so far away they can't even fathom its source, but they quickly discard it and return to the surface to deal with the seemingly important aspects of everyday life that crowd their inbox. Years pass, their children have children, and every time they gaze out that window, those old dreams flood their minds again. Big dreams. Dreams they're afraid to try to reach, but yet linger. They may think they're too fat or too old or what-ever their excuse is, they all have an excuse that prevents them from reaching those dreams. If a fifty-two year old, slightly fat man can swim the Amazon, what can you do? Those last two hours before sunset can often be the best swimming of the day.

ACKNOWLEDGMENTS

Exploration of the world's most unreachable places has become quite popular and challenging in the last decades. Some climb Everest, some sail around the world, some walk to the North and South poles, and some row across the oceans.

In recent years I've been rolled by a wave of dreams that inspired me to attempt to swim the world greatest rivers. The Amazon, the largest, longest, and most dangerous river, was always my biggest dream. I did not only swim the Amazon to achieve some great record or sport result, but also much more. I decided to do it with the mission to show the world something different, something really important for our present and future living. We have to protect our forests to keep them growing. We need to keep rivers and other waters clean. The world is still a beautiful place; we need to protect it and keep it that way for future generations. This issue is bigger than any of us alone can comprehend. The future of mankind depends on us.

I was not strong enough to swim the river all by myself; I had a talented team to support me. I decided to risk my life for this gruelling project, which shook up the world and made history. Without the right hard-working people around me, this would be an impossible mission. I would like to thank all of the people who I was fortunate to have around me, those who suffered and laughed with me, and contributed their own part to this unforgettable project.

Here, I would like to thank and name the following people, companies, and institutions that helped make my challenge possible. Without the names on this little dedicated space at the end of the book, this project would not be possible.

Swim team
Borut Strel (expedition leader), Matthew Mohlke (river navigator, book and journal writer), Bojan Premelc (Pibi) (tech support), Valter Stepan (river navigator), Jamie Zelazny (river navigator), Corrado Filipponi (photographer).

Technical team
The IIN Group of Companies, (Yoram Yaeli, Aldo Souza, Andre Luiz Souza).

Medical team
Amazon Virtual Medical Team (AVMT) members with Prof. Rifat Latifi, MD, FACS (medical director); Dr. Mateja de Leonni Stanonik, MD, PhD (team's physician), University of Arizona and University of Tennessee (Knoxville).

Boat crews
Peruvian part: Alfredo Chavez (boat captain), Paul Wright (boat owner), the boat crew members on the *Cielito Lindo* boat.

Brazilian part: Miguel Rocha da Silva (boat captain), the boat crew members on the *Cassiquiari* boat.

Security team
Peruvian and Brazilian Armed Forces and Navy, police officers from Gurupa and Corpo de Bombeiros Militar of the city of Santarém

Film crew and PR office in Los Angeles
Self Pictures production company with John Maringouin (film director), Mickey Cottrell (executive producer), Molly Lynch (producer), Maria Florio (producer), Inclusive PR Company for helping us bring an event to the major worldwide media houses. We hope you all go out and see the movie they've made about the swim. It's called *Big River Man*.

Slovenian Armed Forces
For making contacts to other forces in Peru and Brazil and for borrowing us much needed equipment for our operational mission on the river.

Many thanks to all the cities and states along the river, their mayors and governors. And special thanks to: Mr. Amazonino Armando Mendes (Ex-Governor of the state of Amazonas), Mrs. Ana Julia Carepa (Governor of the state of Para), Mr. Francisco De Asis Mendoza De Souza (province of Atalaya, Peru), Abog. Jorge Velásquez Portocarrero (mayor of Atalaya, Peru), Mr. Carlos Henderson (businessman in Pucallpa, Peru), Alex Ayuli (TII Worldwide).

Project sponsors and supporters:

The IIN Group of Companies, VBrick Systems, C.Foster, Ses New Skies, Santa Cláudia, Nes Sportswear, Speedo-Spectra International, Orca Performance, Lenovo, Energizer, Chaco, BlueSeventy, Kelty, Tender Corporation, Zoll-advancing resuscitation, General Devices, Second Opinion Software, Slovenian Tourist Organization, Amazon Comunicáo Belém, Kompas Telecommunications, Trival antene, Protechnik, Kliping, Interseek, Internet Peterka, Siol, Petrol, Prevent Global, Btc City, Krka, Lek, Litostroj, Metropolis, Triglav, TCG Unitech, Trimo, Dnevnik, Kompas, GMM, Mazda, Ministry Of Defence Slovenia, Bank of Koper, Interevropa, Postojna cave, Tanin, Autocommerce, Municipality of Novo Mesto, Municipality of Ptuj, Municipality of Trebnje, Municipality of Grosuplje, McDonald's Slovenia, Elektro Maribor, Elektro Ljubljana, Primorje, Kobra Team, Hotel Slon, Polar-Intact Group, Planet of Health, Svea, A Net, Gorenjka, Nivo Celje, Tkanina, Tekstil, The Celje Fair, Cvicek Wine Krsko, Perspektiva, Lipacom, Splosna Plovba Shipping, Mercator, Tivoli Swimming Pools, Smarjeske Toplice Spa Resort, Medica Artis, Kolpa san, Grafex.

No amount of thanks is adequate when it comes to Matthew Mohlke, my expedition partner and companion, for his persistence and hard work. We have been together day after day on many expeditions since Mississippi 2002. We have endured many difficult and dangerous times together but came away the closest friends. Our book is the truest testimony to the success of the Amazon expedition.

I would also like to thank my other book partners, Michael Ellsberg, the greatest editor I have ever seen, and our efficient literary agent, Margaret Gee from Australia.

Thanks to my family, my wife Nusa, and daughter Nina for their unconditional support toward my dreams, even though it meant my being away from home for months and months.

Special thanks to my biggest partner and most effective man in my team, my son Borut. Without him, I would not be able to achieve what I did. He has been my support, leader, manager, designer, actor, and PR guy from day one of the planning of the expedition, and never doubted my success for even a moment. He is a phenomenon at the age of twenty-six, and deserves the label, "He is the Man" forever.

Finally, I'd like to thank all of you who followed my progress on the website and other news media. Your kind letters and cheers from the shoreline kept me going through the most painful moments of the swim. Thank you so much; I'm not sure if I could have made it without all of your encouragement. I swim for peace, friendship, and clean waters. Please do your part to preserve these gifts for future generations.

Thank you very much,

Martin Strel